WTF I'M TRYING TO BE SPIRITUAL

A GUIDEBOOK FOR LOVING YOURSELF WITHOUT FEAR

JEANETTE BISHOP AND HELEN VARGA

authorHOUSE°

AuthorHouse™
1663 Liberty Drive
Bloomington, IN 47403
www.authorhouse.com
Phone: 1 (800) 839-8640

Published by AuthorHouse 06/01/2016

ISBN: 978-1-4918-4558-5 (sc)
ISBN: 978-1-4918-4557-8 (hc)
ISBN: 978-1-4918-4758-9 (e)

Library of Congress Control Number: 2013923124

Print information available on the last page.

Any people depicted in stock imagery provided by Thinkstock are models,
and such images are being used for illustrative purposes only.
Certain stock imagery © Thinkstock.

This book is printed on acid-free paper.

Because of the dynamic nature of the Internet, any web addresses or links contained in
this book may have changed since publication and may no longer be valid. The views
expressed in this work are solely those of the author and do not necessarily reflect the
views of the publisher, and the publisher hereby disclaims any responsibility for them.

Contents

PART IV - THE HUMAN RACE

PART V - FULL CIRCLE

Self-Love Introduction

WHAT IF OUR DILEMMAS COULD be solved by a single concept? We—Jeanette and Helen—have asked Spirit many questions throughout the years. Why do people lie down and have sex in rooms filled with feces, urine, and litter? Why do we have disease and health problems? One answer would appear consistently. Spirit's reply was, "A lack of love." Imagine our surprise when we were told that many detrimental acts affecting our well-being were attempts to bring about love and compassion for ourselves. Hence, everything has a spiritual answer.

Yet, life is not meant to be a huge spiritual revelation on a daily basis. Life is meant to be lived and experienced to the best of our ability. However, in today's world, it seems that our "good" is never quite good enough. Many of us seek validation externally through relationships, competitiveness, victimization, perfectionism, or materialism, which may lead some to addictions or obsessions. Many people doubt their self-worth and as a result seek comfort in externals. They do so in the hope of finding the unconditional love they never received from those they loved and trusted the most, hoping to fill the void of feelings of unlovedness toward themselves. Hence, it boils down to the very essence of feeling disconnected from the power of love. Just by expressing mere anger or hatred, we separate ourselves from that love. The bottom line is that we disengage from love, whether we disconnect from our own sense of self-love or from our own sense of love and compassion toward other human beings.

We aren't reinventing the wheel here; we are reinventing you and me. This book isn't about angel dust, fairy fluff, or pixie poop, but rather about breaking habits and cycles that we act out, either consciously or unconsciously. It concerns stopping your own cycle of inner babble that takes you on a negative tangent, where in order to feel good about yourself or feel superior, you put someone else down through criticism. This gives you a spark of energy that creates a high, but you only feel good for a short period. When you come down from that temporary buzz, you crash, once again feeling negative and guilty while saying to yourself, "Oh, I'm not a good person." In actuality, we are all "perfect" in our own right, without having to be negative toward others.

Hence, it is our attempt—through Spirit's wisdom—to give God's message of love to all the wounded hearts in this world seeking solace and wishing to find a way to turn that self-loathing into self-love and to know that they are loved and loveable. God accepts us, regardless of how we choose to experience ourselves, our divinity, higher power, life force, unconditional love, soul, spirit, self, intuition, essence, gut feeling, or however you deem it. Everyone will call it by different names and have different ideas as to what it may actually be. What is important is whatever is true for you (which may change and evolve over time). It is your experiential journey.

You are the spiritual experience! Each one of us is an expression of God. Hence, there are no paths leading to God, because God is always right there in front of you, knocking on your heart. God is waiting for you to open that door to the awareness of who you really are and share that expression with the world. Of course, it becomes difficult when we are distracted by the chaos that we call life (including work, family, media, technology, politics, religion, and the like). Success comes from having a relationship with ourselves and with that aspect within our being, regardless if one believes in God. Furthermore, it's difficult to have balance in our lives if we're unhappy within ourselves. Loving yourself will reveal that beauty within. As a result, the most popular question Jeanette's clients would ask during Spirit communication and clairvoyant message work was, "How do I love myself?" It would seem this lack of love has been a recurring theme, both in our lives and the lives of others.

Jeanette herself has experienced abuse as a child, rape as a teenager, a teenage pregnancy, and homelessness. She has walked the walk of abuse, violence, and poverty. The death of her two-year-old son led her to question God and life's apparent cruelty and suffering. These tragedies caused her to look further than the experiences themselves, and Spirit's wisdom and love helped her understand the greater meaning of our everyday life.

In contrast, Helen's personal understanding of God as being her equal from a tender age eroded via her upbringing as an only child in a competitive, patriarchal family that included a strict Catholic background. Consequently, this caused her to doubt her personal encounters with God, leading her to experience self-hatred and question God's love and motives.

The two of us have gone through mental and emotional upheavals, with the anxiety and fear of day-to-day living. This has included cyclic patterns of guilt and shame, which have been fraught with anger, sadness, and hopelessness. We have experienced our share of suffering and the self-mutilation of our inner being. However, as we let go of the pain, we felt it necessary to share the advice and information God/Spirit has given us through the years. Some readers might be offended and angry, some inspired, while others may find themselves receiving a spiritual bitch slap, so to speak, from within these pages. We expect to raise some eyebrows and maybe even make some enemies. What matters is this: we want the world to know, one heart at a time, that self-love *really* is important. So read on, giggle, or rant if you must, but give it a shot.

(Just a note to our readers that any repetitive material, as well as what appears to be improper sentence structure and grammar, is a result of the way information was received via God/Spirit and not a lack of editorial oversight. This book is not intended to diagnose, prescribe, or replace medical and professional care (physician, psychiatrist, psychologist, therapist, counselor, and the like). If you are experiencing any type of emotional distress, mental health issues, and/or physical problems, we urge you to seek the proper medical and professional aid (advice, care, and/or treatment) you may need in order to heal.)

HELEN: How will the reader benefit from this book?

JEANETTE/UNIVERSAL SOURCE: Because of its truth that it holds. Just as in the same way that the Bible, Kabbalah, or Torah reveals truths in the script that it uses, in essence the script of the English language that you are using brings truth. Truth benefits, regardless of language, and it is the English language you are using in order to communicate. With communication, regardless of creed, color, language, or any kind of barrier, it doesn't matter because truth resonates. It always does. Whether it stays outside the person and their energy and filters in slowly or whether they get it right at that moment and the light bulb goes on—they will benefit. It will benefit all areas of their lives because they are not just one entity with one dimension. You are a spiritual human being with many dimensions—be it physical, mental, emotional, intellectual, spiritual, or sexual—on all of those levels, it will filter in, because whatever you read, you're not just taking it in as a physical being—you're actually taking that in on all levels of your energy levels.

HELEN: Many of the concepts in the book come from a source that cannot be explained. What if people do not believe in God or Spirit?

JEN/UNIVERSAL SOURCE: It doesn't really matter if a person believes in God or Spirit, because God and Spirit is the same thing. The beauty about that is that they [God and Spirit] don't have to be right, so they don't need to put that across as though they're saying to the universe, "Well we're right and you're wrong." It's not about that. Therefore, God and Spirit are not about being "right." It is just about revealing truth. That's all there is to it. So whether you believe in it or not, the truth will still resonate [regardless] at some point in a person's life because that's how it works—be it emotionally, mentally, physically, spiritually, sexually, or intellectually. It doesn't matter. Somewhere in that person's being, the truth will resonate because it will make sense—it will not be "nonsense." It's not as if we—God and Spirit—are saying, "Well you have to believe it this way in order for it to work." Not so. It's all about revealing LOVE within for their own selves and being able to share that LOVE with other beings. In essence, LOVE is light; it shines regardless. It is always there; we have moments of receiving that unconditional LOVE that is light, and we have those things happen to us regardless of what we believe in, because LOVE is LOVE.

The other aspect of that is it is not an arrogant way of thinking. It's just saying, "It's okay if you don't believe in God or Spirit." It doesn't matter if you feel that way, because there is no right or wrong way to validate yourselves and the universe. It's not about stating, "If you don't believe this, then you're wrong." The universe presents us with LOVE at every level, at anytime, anywhere, wherever we are willing to accept that. It will keep shining whether we're willing to accept that or not. Again, it doesn't matter. It keeps flowing. Whatever the human being decides to do, God and Spirit are fine with that, because it's all part of a learning curve. It's all about bringing those experiences "home." That's what it's really about—becoming more enlightened and how we deal with each other. It's not about, "you have bad karma," so now you'll have bad karma coming to you all the time. If you believe that, then that's what is going to happen. If you want to create that, go ahead; no one is going to stop you.

It's not about being arrogant. It's about allowing the person free will and choice to choose whatever they desire. If they choose LOVE over hate, then wonderful. If they choose hate, then that's part of their creation. It is just another aspect of LOVE. Therefore, it really doesn't matter.

HELEN: Can God expand on "hate is just another aspect of love"?

JEN/UNIVERSAL SOURCE: We live in a world of opposites. That's apparent because we oppose one another as human beings. We oppose our universal laws when we hurt each other or hurt our Earth. So we believe in opposites. If you hate something deeply, it usually means that you have an immense power to love. Therefore, what you're really saying is, "I would really love to love, but I don't trust it, and I don't know how to, so I have to push everything away. I have to oppose many things because I don't understand." What a person is actually saying is they have an immense capacity to love. That's why love and hate are of the same pole. For example, you fill a glass but not quite to the top. Someone says, "It's not full." This is an oppositional statement, one inspired by the need for absolutes. We want positive proof of love; it's about exposure and opposites. When we expose hate, we're allowing love to flow in simply because we've exposed it. If we expose the hatred within ourselves, we do ourselves a great service by allowing that love to flow in. Don't be afraid; you don't have to shout it from the rooftops. Just know yourself so you don't perpetuate your history of pain and suffering. The only judge is you, and this inner judge loves to make you miserable and create the vicious cycle.

Let's clarify this further. Often we hate the very thing which we are capable of ourselves; extreme hatred for war is only because we are aware of our own wars we create, essentially a mirror to our own emotions, thoughts, and sometimes actions too. We hate because of the ignorance we perpetuate. We hate if others don't have the same opinions we do. We desire to love, yet we won't accept that we are not separate—we are all one. It is hard to accept that we are one with a dictator or an abuser, yet if we were to look deep inside, we would find threads of commonality, both positive and negative. It's not easy to hear that you have commonality with someone who perpetuates abuse, for example, your own usage of bullying. It has all the same elements in it and causes just as much damage. How about the horrible things we do to ourselves? For instance, when we tell ourselves that we are stupid, ugly, or worthless, we are using verbal abuse toward ourselves, which is a form of violence in itself. Committing crimes against humanity starts within. It is just different levels and modus operandi.

JEN: I am still peeling back my own stories of hatred and allowing love to flow in.

HEL: Myself included.

Thus, the common thread that weaves through humanity is our lack of love and our efforts to overcome not just the cruelty we face from others but the judge inside ourselves that declares us to be simply "not good enough." We know the answer is to reconnect and to value ourselves enough to stop that devastating self-loathing on all levels of our being: mentally, emotionally, physically, and spiritually. Take what you need as a stepping stone—it could be one sentence or even one word—and disregard what isn't true for you. Even if you do not believe in God, we all have an inner voice within our being. If we listen to it and follow our heart's desire, we will have created our own doctrine, our own truth to live and love by.

PART ONE

EARLY INSIGHTS

Chapter One

The Source of Our Pain

As a child and later a young adult growing up in Scotland, Jeanette frequently conversed with God, often questioning the pain and suffering she witnessed, whether it was her own trials or those of others. As Jeanette matured, God instructed her over a number of years, giving insights as she developed understanding. "Squashing creates a deviation of energy, seeking solace for the pain it causes—an aspirin, if you will; all are seeking love of the unconditional kind," He told her.

"What is it they squash?" Jeanette asked.

"All people squash the feelings of inadequacy, feelings of being unloved, feelings of being unacceptable to others, and even feelings of not belonging to the human race where they live, to name but a few," He informed her.

"Where does this begin, God, and why does it begin?" She brooded while listening to His wisdom.

"Do you remember when you were small, and we talked about the stars and the moon? How you were part of all of that, and everyone else in the world is part of all that?" He asked.

"Yes, I do. I remember that night very well. We lay in the long wheat in the middle of the night and looked up at the stars and the moon. I was upset that night. I had been beaten by my stepmother for blurting out a part of her secret life. I had a hard time with her calling me a liar and conniving. I wanted to understand why I was going through that at that time," she replied.

"Yes, well, it began then and even younger," God gently told her. "Children are innocents, as we all are, even adults. You are conditioned to believe certain things about yourself through your childhood, so you can be controlled and manipulated to the ways of whoever is the authority figure at that time. That is what gives them power and feelings of importance, as you bend to their will."

"Yeah, okay, but why do they do that? You would think they would know better and not want to hurt their future, right?"

"I understand, Jeanette, you would be angry. It is your conditioning that is creating that anger, your pain, and your suffering, as we talked about in the beginning. Are you aware of your pain at this time?" God asked.

"Yes, I am aware," she replied indignantly.

"Are you aware of where this pain is coming from?" God asked gently.

"Yes, of course I am! It comes from the injustice of it all."

"Yes, injustice. It is the injustice part of your childhood and how you felt wrongly accused?" asked God.

"No, I just feel that way about any overpowering of an innocent."

"Could it be you feel that way because you understand what it is to be an innocent and be betrayed by love as you saw it?" God gently asked.

Jeanette broke down; she cried and cried.

"You see, Jeanette, your tears are all your pains coming out, so it isn't suppressed. If suppressed, the energy will find a way to get out. It will seek love, to be soothed and healed. At the first sign of interest or love, it might run into the arms of the lover, often the very same energy of the pain—a mirror, if you will—so it may see itself, release the energy, and heal. However, without understanding, the pain just continues to grow and sabotage itself to pain and suffering again, as it rejects love for power over another, as that is what 'young' feelings of love believe. In order to love, one *must* own the lover; otherwise it is pointless and means you have no power and are weak in some way."

"Oh, my God!" Jeanette was astounded as the knowledge fell into place within her being.

"Yes?" he replied.

His sense of humor is wonderful!

"What do you mean, 'young feelings of love'?" she asked as she replayed the conversation in her head.

"It means, my love, young feelings of love are the feelings of love experienced or want of experience from a young age, which was never given the chance to mature or allowed to experience into adulthood," God answered.

She asked Him exactly what He meant by "never given a chance to mature or allowed to experience."

"It means the emotions a child experiences aren't allowed to grow as they age; they stay at the same age. Emotions will seek a place to grow and mature unconsciously in the mind, although the soul knows the path," was God's reply.

Does that mean, then, if you are traumatized emotionally at age five, those emotions may stay at that level? Yes, it does. God showed Jeanette that when a child is hurt emotionally, the child does not know how to ease that pain, so the pain continues as he or she grows. At some point, in one way or another, it will come to the surface. Looking for the power to feel "good" about oneself, seeking retribution for the pain, or victimizing oneself are all common. One might be rescued from the pain through these methods; however, it is a short-lived remedy, and the pain will frequently rear its ugly head. This happens simply because the understanding is not present and was not taught at a young age.

This does not mean that everyone who has been abused, to varying degrees, will actually perpetrate the same things on others. However, perpetration of a pain and inside hurt can take many forms.

"A person may self-sabotage his or her growth by making decisions based on self-esteem," God told Jeanette. "Another may teach others and indoctrinate others in their ways for power and insist on the 'right' way. These are all stepping stones to greater understanding and growth spiritually, since we are all spirit in flesh."

"What do you mean 'we' are all spirit in flesh? You aren't in the flesh."

"Ah, yes, I wondered if you would catch that. Yes, I am in the flesh, in each and every human being, every flower, every tree, every living thing. I am in the flesh, experiencing the world," was God's reply.

"So when you say *everyone*, does that mean you are experiencing the 'good' person who is being abused or hurt in some way *and* the person who is 'bad'? How can that be?" Jeanette asked, bewildered.

"There is no such thing as separateness in the world of the physical," God gently told her. "I am everywhere and in everything, including the wrongdoers and the righteousness, as you put it. There is no right or wrong; there just *is*, and each situation is the same—the lack of love within and the feelings of being unloved."

PART TWO

THE THREE RULES
OF LOVE

Chapter Two

Who the Hell Am I, Anyway?

"Trust is seeking ourselves externally in an egotistical way because we lack love within ourselves. When we need to trust, or desire to trust, that means it's based on neediness, which means we need something from the person or God in order to be validated of our exclusivity and loved-ness. We need trust from the outside to know we are okay inside, instead of seeking within."

—God, 2001

WE HAVE GIVEN VALUE TO the negative opinions others have thought and said about us since the beginning of our childhood. These opinions and beliefs have left countless individuals with low self-worth and a lack of love for themselves. As a result, they have developed an emotional attachment to these beliefs about themselves and been left searching for the unconditional love they may not have received as children. *Emotions are the chains of the mental beliefs that bind us to our experiences.*

Everything begins with an emotion, which develops into a mental belief as we try to make sense of how we feel; we survive the damage that has been inflicted upon us by others. Lasting impressions from our youth, especially negative imprints, leave us with a need to please, in order to gain some sort of recognition through validation. Adults who create expectations for children to live up to often result in their children feeling unworthy. These adults are obviously working out their own childhood issues regarding feelings of worthiness, and so the cycle perpetuates. It becomes more about what adults want from children, as opposed to creating a relationship based on developing inner trust and love.

In an effort to regain their "love," as we see it through the eyes of a now-adult child, we recreate the scenario throughout our lives in our relationships, in an effort to find ourselves and know we are good enough. Is it possible that we are looking for external validation because we were never taught how to validate ourselves?

Why were some of the people we trusted as children so negative and yet some were very positive? Why were we not always able to hang on to the positive stuff? Could it be that some of us were not taught how to love ourselves as children because the opinions of those we trusted were unquestionable?

Few things are worse than the memories of that big bully who towered over you as a child. The bully can take the shape of parent, teacher, peer, next-door neighbor, family member, or sibling—in fact, just about anyone. That feeling of helplessness and loss of power as a child can render us vulnerable in adult life; relationships can be emotionally chaotic at best.

HEL: "Oh, my God, what's wrong with you? You crazy? You not normal." How many times did I hear those comments from certain members of my family? I became convinced in my later years that I was indeed "not normal" and slowly going insane and should commit myself into a mental hospital. I also remember my uncle telling me more than once, "The older you get, the dumber you get." For a long time, I thought it was some profound Hungarian proverb and took it quite literally. I didn't question my family regarding their beliefs about me; they must have known something I didn't. As an adult, I would ask myself, *"What's wrong with me? Why can't I be like everyone else?"*

JEN: In my house, my step-grandmother always sneaked in on me when I was playing with my toys in my room, making sure I wasn't doing anything "dirty"—whatever that meant. I was five years old, and from then onward, I became obsessed with my own bodily smells. I thought I was the only "dirty" person in our family. I stayed away from people, just in case they could smell me, although I had a hard time finding out exactly what it was I smelled of to begin with. My step-grandmother would always hiss at me, "You know what I am talking about!" It took me years to recognize that my body smells were very normal and there was nothing wrong with me. Unfortunately, I didn't question either, because I was too afraid of her.

Stepping back emotionally only helps us realize that our desire to please the adults during our childhood was used against us to create control over our behavior. We aren't to blame for an adult's lack of control, lack of parenting, or teaching skills. We cannot change what has happened. However, we can alter how we look at it with our self-love.

We have all had times in our childhood when we have been demoralized over our personalities, our physical appearance, talents, skills, intelligence, and most of all, our behavior. For instance, depending on your culture, ridicule is a wonderful way to make sure children comply with society's ideas of acceptable behavior. They are bombarded with information from an early age regarding what is acceptable and what is not. This follows us into adulthood. Think of the outcasts: the homeless, drug addicts, alcoholics, people with mental illness or some form of physical deformities, those with AIDS or leprosy, the starving, and even victims of genocide. They all fall into the popular behavior of scorn and become the topic of our moral superiority.

We can understand intellectually the concepts thus far. However, to know and understand them emotionally, in order to heal and release our pain, is entirely different. The first step, as hard as it is to do, is to *let go!* As a child and as an adult child, it was not your fault if your parents/teachers/siblings/family/next-door neighbors could not get past their own anger and fears to make you feel loved and wanted.

First, ask yourself what you believe about yourself. For example, what do you like or even love about yourself? (This doesn't seem much like letting go, but we'll get to that point, we promise!) Is it your personality, your physical appearance, maybe your creative talents and skills, your intelligence, be it emotional or logical? We aren't talking about what others think; focus on what *you* think about you. Compare this list with the things you don't like about yourself. Which one seems longer?

Once you listen to the negative beliefs, you can write them down and ask yourself, "Is this valid?" Some might be—for instance, if you cut someone off in traffic, and they call you a nasty name, because a fear of crashing might cause anyone to lash out. However, if the negative belief is something like, "I'm so stupid. I can never do anything right," then you just know it was about meeting an expectation placed on you as a child by someone whom you trusted, admired, or feared. Then we wonder why we have this desire to be perfect. There seems to be a measuring stick for perfection, yet the standard of perfection seems to vary from person to person. For example, what one person considers the perfect pie crust may be deemed by another as ordinary.

That's just a pie crust! Just think how the idea of what constitutes perfection affects everything from romantic relationships to friendships or the workplace.

Some set their standards very high for themselves and the everyday things they do. As a result, they never quite get it right, or they may give up long before they realize they have the potential to become great in their own way, at their own thing.

Letting go of those negative opinions, which have become part of your daily thinking, isn't easy. Making a list of them and putting the name of the person responsible beside the opinion can help you see that your negative opinion isn't the result of your thoughts at all, but rather the thoughts of a person who was obviously unhappy with him- or herself and wanted to feel some sort of power or control over something—*you!*

Once you notice that some things you have believed about yourself aren't real, you may wish to be aware when these negative subtleties arise. Any situation that brings about stress and fear will contribute to your feelings of low self-worth and lack of self-love. Once you have started to break through, you will notice that many negative beliefs will arise in every aspect of your being. Becoming aware and making your journey less stressful are the keys to self-love and happiness within. Opening yourself to the power of reason and understanding can be a great tool to use; hence, you can buy a journal and keep track of your thoughts with the following headings:

What's the belief you have about yourself?
Who told you?
Where are you right now?
How did you get there?
Why does it serve you?

Is it time to release yourself from places or people that feed into that belief? This is one question to ask. The next questions are: *Can* I release myself, and do I *want* to release myself? It takes courage to believe in ourselves and break that cycle of pain. Letting go isn't always easy. However, it helps to remind yourself that the negative opinions you say to yourself aren't yours. They are an illusion made yours.

"An illusion made yours" means any kind of opinion you have developed over the years due to negative behavior that has been presented to you that you've been forced to take on board as your own. For instance, your authority figure (mother, father, or uncle) or someone who had an effect on you emotionally may have kept saying every time they dropped something, "See, if you hadn't kept talking, I wouldn't have done that. It's your fault."

Then you start to look inward and think it's all about you and how you're the one who causes all the problems. You're raised with the illusion that you're at fault for every bad thing that happens. Since you're only a child at the time, it seems to you like you *are* at fault for every bad thing. You have a limited view or window that you look through as a child, whereas an adult has a larger view. Therefore, a child with a limited view would see *everything* that he or she does as being wrong and therefore become convinced that he or she is worthless or stupid. The child would then think, *My mom was right. I am worthless.*

It's not true—it's the illusion that's been made yours. Illusions we keep that are hurtful to our well-being are the ones we decide to own and use to our detriment. Don't keep them! Throw them out every day with the garbage. Define who you are by your own learning curve, and keep growing into who you truly are. This can be achieved through creative thinking and actions, including learning new habits that are great for your self-esteem. Start by loving yourself on special occasions, and then develop that into daily love. Just keep growing into the real *you!* There is absolutely no one like you on this Earth, no replica that is better or worse than you are. *You are unique!* So why waste time trying to be someone else?

Take good care of yourself while you ponder the questions. Remember that these questions are no substitute for counseling or seeking professional help. Don't be ashamed if you require a little support or even a lot of support. At the end of the day, your mental and emotional well-being are much more important than anyone's opinion. If you find yourself in distress over the questions, we urge you to seek proper medical care.

Don't expect that answers will come to you right away; they might, but they may also take a couple of days. It's important not to force the answers. Everything comes in its own time, so have patience.

You started with the questions about what you like or love about yourself. Don't worry if you haven't come up with any answers yet. Let's take it a step further.

In your childhood, did you grow up with positive regard, meaning hugs, kisses, or praise? Did the adults around you show outward affection? Do you remember who did give you loving and supportive encouragement? During childhood, who had the greatest influence on you in terms of love—a grandparent, parent, or teacher? What was impressed upon you most by this significant person?

Do you remember any unloving comments made to you by any family members that still affect you to this day? Isn't it amazing how, in some families, there are concerns that giving a compliment or praise might lead to vanity or conceit? Meanwhile, the same family will take all the credit for their kids' achievements, as if the adults achieved them. Yes, genetics play a part, but without the child's focus, success is impossible. Do you recall any other individual giving you praise or compliments for anything you did?

During childhood, we are greatly affected by our world and who rules it. Thinking of this, recollect who had the greatest positive influence on you by the way they loved you. Can you remember the details of how they made you feel? What was the lasting impression they left on you?

We understand that not everyone had individuals in their lives who were a positive influence on their self-esteem; other coping mechanisms might have been used instead. We both used animals to find love, comfort, and solace. We also found these comforts in nature. There's something about the outdoors that can bring peace to one's inner being.

Religion can also play a part in our childhood development. Some religions put emphasis on imperfections; some treat women as if they were a lesser species. Think of how you view God, for example, as a father figure, punisher, or judge.

Did religion play a part in your outlook toward love for others and love for yourself? If so, ask yourself what your religion taught you about love in a positive regard or a negative regard. Do you recall any type of religious events, practices, or rituals that may have sent you into a spin regarding your self-love and worth, leaving you with a feeling of never quite "making the grade" spiritually? Obviously, there are some wonderful teachings within religion. Can you recall any that might bring about a sense of peace, love, and hope within you?

Going further into our childhoods, we remembered some kids who loved to be in school, because they found a place of safety there. It was one place they knew they could be safe from abuse, and at least they knew what to expect from the school. For some, school was a place they could play, have fun, sing, draw, disappear into great books, be with their best buddies in whom they could confide, and find a shoulder to cry on and lean on.

For others, school brought further blows to the self-esteem, rather than being a pleasant place or a nurturing environment for a child. Yet, these children would have to be there day after day, suffering and lonely. In your experience, how were your school days, and what impact did they make on your self-esteem?

At times, we go broaden our horizons with what we have gained through our education, because something we did made us feel good and proud of ourselves. Remembering these instances can enhance our self-love and bring us back to feelings of self-worth. What was yours, or did you have one? Can you bring to mind any of your favorite subjects in school? Did anyone encourage you in those subjects, and if so, did you cultivate those skills into areas of interest today?

Participating in extracurricular activities is also important for our well-being. It releases stress and transports us to a place of happiness. Children love extracurricular activities. Imagine all that curiosity and sense of wonder bundled up inside of you! Can you remember your favorite extracurricular activity, the one you most loved? In contrast, maybe you were totally discouraged to participate in that activity you desired. Can you remember the reason given to you?

Lasting impressions of a positive time often leave us, as adults, with a yearning for that bygone time, trying to recapture those feelings of worthiness. What lasting impressions are you left with as an adult? Are they a mixed bag of good and bad? Do you have more bad than good? We hope you have more good-quality impressions than negative ones.

The emotional impact of our childhoods can play important roles in how we deal with daily life as adults, especially if there was no explanation given to help us understand what was happening. Today, we obsess about how we look and who we are, based on opinions of the masses and opinions said to us when we were kids. Some of us can work through it by using level-headed thinking; others of us are left scarred. Can you remember if you were taunted at school or in any other area of your life as a child? What impact do you think it has today that affects you consistently? Intimidation, bullying, taunting, and teasing can leave a child wondering where he or she fits in. Sometimes we have a special friend who helps us through that particularly difficult time, one who was positive, helpful, and gave us a shoulder to cry on, someone who actually believed in us. Can you think of a friend who was like that for you? Can you recollect the positive influence that friend has had on you to this day?

It's interesting to note how we base our self-perception on our physical appearance. With the media bombarding us with images of models and celebrities, we are in competition to be someone else. The desire to look a certain way can affect how we look after our health—strenuous exercising, near starvation, or deprivation of certain foods (except chocolate). It may leave us contemplating plastic surgery because we don't like the size of our nose, just because Auntie Faye said so. Do you pick a different body part to hate every week?

Often we have a preconceived notion about our body image because of others' beliefs and views. It may be from your family's past comments or statements from well-meaning friends, neighbors, teachers, the bus driver, or even the cashier at the grocery store; comments such as, "You don't look well today," or "What did you do to yourself? You look different somehow," leave us feeling deflated, especially if we were feeling good that day. Let's not forget the media. The whole world seems to have an opinion about us and our looks.

Is there any correlation between what was said to you as a child regarding your appearance and the way you feel about your physical looks today? Is there a parallel between any comments made regarding your physical appearance as a youngster and to your eating or exercise habits now? Feelings of not making the grade physically can leave us in our own personal nightmare, where our only company is our misery and hatred of who we are and what we look like.

JEN: I suffered from anorexia as a young adult, trying to keep up with my then-boyfriend/husband, who regularly told me I should be little, since I was only five feet two inches tall. I exercised and dieted beyond the norm, to the point of starvation. I was happy when I could buy clothes that would fit a child! I didn't know what "normal" women looked like; I had no idea whatsoever about my body or what it was supposed to look like. To me, everything about it was ugly. Yet, poring over old photographs, I realize that I was simply beautiful, and I wish now that I knew it then. My face and skin were radiant, my eyes wide and bright, my lips always in a smile; straight teeth, a curvy body with long legs, nice ankles. I could wear just about anything. In spite of that, I could only see the faults that everyone told me I had.

Let's reiterate. Go back to the negative thoughts that you have about yourself, and see whose opinion you are hearing. Think of everything, including your appearance, your behavior, your skills and abilities, your intelligence, your emotional capacity, your mental capacity, your physical structure, your masculinity or femininity. Can you identify the person who makes these judgments? How do they relate to you now? Can you let it go? Do you understand that these opinions are meant to make you feel bad? This way, you are manipulated and controlled, so you cannot be who you feel you are, simply because someone else deems it so!

JEN/UNIVERSAL SOURCE: Do not allow others to define who you are.
Say to yourself, "Their opinion matters not." Acceptance [of yourself] is an inner
allowance of your being; resistance sets the mind thinking all sorts of things other
than what you are attempting to achieve. When you resist [loving yourself], your
mind starts to run, and soon, all your feelings and thoughts have meaning; and
before long, the negative voice starts its journey through your body and mind.

Allow all thoughts to pass through your mind. Remain calm, bringing yourself back to the present moment, and be aware if you are projecting either into the future or the past. Attachment to these thoughts is not required right now. Breathe deeply, and sigh upon exhaling. Relax as best you can. If you have a partner, have him or her massage your shoulders; feel the joy in your body at being released from tension. This is why massage is a great thing—your body rejoices at being released from its tension and lack of love. Connection with each other is just another way of loving and being.

JEN/UNIVERSAL SOURCE: Spirit is pure love. (That's why it can go
through any object—a door, a wall—it's such a high vibration.)
Love is so strong that plants grow [reach] upward, even though we have
gravity. Plants do not know any differently because they love what they do and
what they are—being!
Energy never dies; it can change in vibration, frequency, or density. You
cannot stop it or block it; (it's either deviated or repressed). It comes in varying
speeds and forms. It can be the total opposite of itself, for example dense [tangible]
as opposed to intangible. There are different forms of energy: the seen forms, which
are matter, and the unseen forms, which are vibration. If you take a piece of
wood, it's reverberating at a lower speed; therefore, it becomes condensed. Thus,
it is matter.
Each one of us has a frequency. It changes when we die; it becomes subtle.
When someone is happy, sad, or angry, you feel that person's frequency. You
transmit energy; you emit it, and you receive it. We're transmitters and receivers.
Pain is an energy.
We humans suppress ourselves; we lack love for ourselves. Hence, we created
gravity in the belief that we needed to be kept down. We are spirit made flesh;
we have many different vibrations. To expand your energy [vibrations/frequency]
practice non-judgment. All energies are manifestations of various forms of love. It
will mean different things to different people based upon their experiences. LOVE
vibrates at a high speed.

We are plugged into the universe/soul all the time. Your brain is the circuitry; the switch is you being awake from coming out of the egotistical sabotage, while your soul is the transformer. Hence, our thoughts are living. Thoughts are an event that takes place when our consciousness is sparked into movement. They can be expressed in some form, be it emotionally or physically, such as language; then in some form it manifests.

When you change your thoughts, they change the way they route in the neural system, and hence their energy is changed as well; they also change the amount they love, for instance, by giving and receiving more.

You're trying to re-circuit your brain so you can see, hear, and feel Spirit.

You become aware of Spirit when your mind starts to quiet down, as you allow your filters to fall away, and soon your senses are awake! You become a silent witness and an antenna for the energies unseen. This doesn't mean going into an altered state; it just means you have allowed yourself to feel in a way other than the level you usually do, which in most cases is the pain mode: anguish, suffering, anger, unhappiness, bargaining, manipulating, and so on. These emotions are not "bad"; they just *are.* They exist to remind you to wake up to Spirit and allow yourself to be the real you! They are triggers to wake you up.

*JEN/UNIVERSAL SOURCE: *The more you feel the emotions of pain and suffering, like anguish, anger, unhappiness, the more you are creating further pain and suffering, which is like healing in actual fact, if you allow the feelings to be rerouted into feelings of love and peace.*

Much like a cut—in order for it to heal, you have to clean out the dirt and debris from the cut. It is painful and feels raw. (We feel something like this when we are learning to trust ourselves and rid ourselves of the frame of reference of pain.) Once the cut is clean and a Band-Aid is placed on the wound, it is covered so the new skin can grow. During this time, our bodies go to immense work to bring our cell intelligence to the wound in order to heal it.

Our love within does the exact same thing, as soon as we resist the need to be angry or experience some negative emotion, it is like a healing call to the love. As we resist [the cleaning out of the wound], it is painful as we feel the "need" to feel and say the emotions of pain as a way of cleansing and getting rid of the energy behind it, which has now saturated our cells and sent our bodies into fight-or-flight mode. It is a habit, much like an addiction. The love floods into our minds, our brains change the way it is receiving the messages and modes of anger into those of peace and relaxation [the Band-Aid part]. Love floods through the body and mind, and soon healing begins and the disaster of fear and foreboding has been replaced with new expressions and thoughts.

Therefore, you can now understand that you are becoming awake. Being kind to yourself and to others around you encourages the gift of love within you to grow. Love isn't bought or sold; you cannot bargain for it. You can only allow it to surface.

It may take a little time, and this is the time you need to remind yourself that instant gratification based upon dysfunctional mental and emotional states creates egotistical sabotage. Waking up from these illusions can be a scary thing!

JEN/UNIVERSAL SOURCE: Instant gratification is nothing like fulfillment, although it is in many ways. You can feel fulfillment instantly, but it isn't long-lasting.

Think of a favorite food, say, chocolate. You dream it, you crave it, even if you know it will not do you any good whatsoever. You might get a migraine from eating a chocolate bar, or you might feel bad as you are trying to eat healthy.

You eat the chocolate bar, you savor it and delight in the fact your senses are just whirling in a state of ecstasy over the chocolate bar. The moment is gone in a flash, and that is instant gratification. It only lasts a moment, hence why addictions are so difficult to heal. The momentary high one gets from chocolate, drugs, cigarettes, and the like sends the mind into pleasure mode almost immediately.

So you might think that waking up spiritually is a waste of time and go for more illusionary ways to create a so-called spiritual experience, or you might feel you aren't going anywhere after say, one or two tries. This is the way of the mind, which is used to only thinking one way, or perhaps in ways that aren't entirely healthy for you, to derail you in your task to loving yourself wholly. When your mind is in the habit of thinking one way, it is expected that the mind will resist.

Loving yourself enough to allow yourself time to find your direction, and not to expect instant results which will gratify that sense of perfectionism, is possibly one of the kindest acts you can perform for yourself during your journey.

[With the exception of a few areas that are marked by an asterisk indicating information received during 2008 from the Universal Source, some of the above material in this section was written in 2001 and

subsequent years, as received by Jeanette. It also includes the knowledge Jeanette received from God during the many years prior to those dates. This means as the soul grows, so does the person, and his or her knowledge increases with the openness to receive. Therefore, information received from God in the past will change and evolve.]

CHAPTER THREE

DAMN IT—I DESERVE!

Do you feel your family and friends want the best for you? Does what they want match with what you want for yourself? How many times do you actually just *settle* for less than you really think you desire? Compare your wishes with what your friends and family desire for you in a romantic relationship, as well as a career, home, family, friends, financial stability, health, and the like. Sometimes our friends and family can see that we are settling for less than what we truly deserve. For example, we decide that our heart's desire is to marry a person who may not be right for us, and our family can see it isn't in our best interests. Then there's the other side, when our family wants us to marry the person they deem acceptable and "right" for us, maybe because of financial status, and we do it to please them.

Sometimes our view can become blurry if we live our lives through the eyes and opinions of our family, leaving us with a sense of unfulfilled dreams and yearning for a life unrealized. Following our desires may create fearfulness in those close to us. They may think that somehow they will become unworthy of our attention if we become rich, famous, or better than them somehow (even though that's not the case), because we've made it (whatever that means to each of us) and are happy. Consequently, people often become martyrs to their friends and family for fear of hurting them. For instance, someone might tell you, "Don't you dare take that once-in-a-lifetime job promotion to Australia, because Mom might just die of loneliness." No one is suggesting for a moment that one ought to walk on others to get to where one desires to be. However, sometimes we can be riddled with guilt when we contemplate following our bliss. Our guilt and shame for wanting something more can block our creativity toward achieving great things. It makes no sense whatsoever to deny our very existence and all the good experiences we can bring about for ourselves.

Furthermore, loving those experiences—be they good, bad, or neutral—is not always easy. However, we can only change our own daily perceptions by not judging them in a critical or unfavorable manner. How can we do that? It's hard not to judge something if it is hurtful or damaging to our well-being in some way. This is where healthy boundaries come in—mentally, emotionally, physically, spiritually, or anywhere else in our being.

Experiences give us knowledge of who we are; how we react to them will shape the history of our lives and give us insights to use for our benefit. Thus, knowledge becomes wisdom applied. For example, if we make decisions that seem, in hindsight, a tad aggressive, we can reflect and think of different ways to deal with the situation if it comes around again.

Our sense of love can be somewhat warped in our society, because of our thoughts being linked to conditional love and poor spiritual values, which may carry us through daily life. This, in turn, means we are judging our experiences mainly in a negative way. Finding beauty and seeing the positive in most situations brings us to balance. This lets us know that the energy of the Earth is far greater than we could imagine, and the energy of life has its own rules to follow. Think of the seasons—life, death, and rebirth; renewal always follows a period of destruction, as when spring emerges following a dark winter. Spirit always reminded us that even when it rains, the sun is shining somewhere. In addition, we can remember that the plant life of our world must love us, because they transform our pollutants into life-giving oxygen.

We cohabit with our world, and if we look at it during our lowest ebb, we can remind ourselves, "Whatever my frame of reference is right now, be it from another person or a situation I'm in, I have to change that frame of reference when I look at the world, because there's a bigger picture here. My world isn't all about this tiny, little perspective." It's just one experience out of a day or one out of several years; our lifespan is much bigger than that.

If you have difficult times for several years, it can bring you down, *but only if you allow it to.* You can actually change the way you think and say, "How did I get back here again? I need to step out of this situation I'm in and see the beauty around me and know there are greater forces at work here than I could possibly ever imagine. All I have to do is keep creating the positive."

No one is saying it's easy to do, but once you get into the habit, it becomes easier. You start to realize that our anxiety-driven state can be caused by many factors: pollutants in our food, air, and water; people we relate to; the hurried pace of life, influenced by mass media; or our own insecurities, because we feel we have to be perfect at everything. All of those things combined can create anxiety within a person, causing him or her to react because of something beyond his or her control.

Honestly, we have no control over most of our lives. We can only control how we review them and how we represent ourselves. We can choose to see the beauty and the good in things and say to ourselves, "What's this situation teaching me right now? Where can I go with this situation that will bring me to a better place?"

When you relax your mind, the answers come, because this is what you're creating: a space for the answers to come. If you can do that, you will find yourself in a better place almost immediately. Even if it's for a split second, at least you've experienced it, which is better than no experience at all.

CHAPTER FOUR

LIMITS VERSUS LIMITLESSNESS: KNOW YOUR BOUNDARIES

As CHILDREN, MANY OF US have experienced the destruction of our boundaries, sometimes on a consistent basis by those we trusted. As adults, some of us find it difficult to re-establish our boundaries in a safe and meaningful way. Either we run roughshod over others, or we allow ourselves to be trampled. We may be left in pain, with feelings of anger that mask hurt, sadness, shame, fear, or even guilt. How many times have we been afraid to establish boundaries with others, out of fear of confrontation or possible rejection?

Sometimes we may expect another person to "know" how to behave toward us. Unfortunately, people are not mind-readers; therefore, guidelines or boundaries that clearly state "this is as far as you can go" protect our well being—be it mental, physical, emotional, spiritual, or sexual. Remembering how loving we can be within our boundaries will only enhance life itself; allowing others to continue their negative behavior toward us only shows a lack of respect and dignity for oneself.

To make things clearer, let's have a look at the different types of boundaries you can experience for your own well-being and the limits you would like to establish with yourself and others. Personal boundaries we set for ourselves are also important, because they are a reflection on how we value our own being. So where do you draw the line? Here are some examples.

My physical boundaries:
> No one is allowed to hit or harm me.
> I listen to my body and rest when I need to.

My mental boundaries:
> Individuals are *not* permitted to degrade my intelligence.
> I will not validate the inner critic within me.

My emotional boundaries:
> I will *not* allow anyone to use guilt to manipulate me.
> I will show compassion toward myself.

My spiritual boundaries:
> I will be meditating for five minutes; please do *not* interrupt.

My sexual boundaries:
> I am allowed to express myself sexually and enjoy my body
> the way I wish to, without harm to myself or others, as a
> consensual adult with other consensual adults.

These examples are just guidelines for you to start your own creative process. How easily you set your boundaries will depend on how you take the steps to create them. Going slowly is always a great way to start, as you get used to actually being more respectful toward yourself and others.

Personally, we go by two lists: the Put Up with Your Shit list and the No Fucking Way list, which allows us to recognize who we would give special dispensations and those we wouldn't. Our No Fucking Way list also showed us whom we were "afraid" of and helped us develop courage dealing with this. Just remember that if a person on your Put Up with Your Shit list invades your comfort zone, put them on your No Fucking Way list until they get the message to respect you. It doesn't mean you don't love them anymore; according to Spirit, you may just need to love them from a distance instead. Maybe if you can step away from people like that, you might find there is a completely new world out there that just loves to show you that *you deserve.*

Whereas establishing boundaries with others helps in maintaining our integrity, setting strict boundaries for ourselves may, in fact, prevent us from moving forward. Limiting ourselves may cause us to miss out on different experiences we wish to have, as well as expansion on many levels—intellectual, emotional, physical, and spiritual. What keeps you from breaking out of your mental construct, the same old way of thinking about and doing things? Could it be the fear of criticism or rejection, of failure or success, of making a mistake? Alternatively, is it a fear of the unknown or of trusting your own judgment? Is it a belief that you don't deserve the best the universe has to offer? Do any of these hold true for you? Maybe you can come up with a few of your own.

There are no limits to what you deserve based on integrity, whether it's your physical, mental, or emotional well-being. This encompasses all aspects of daily living, including relationships, career, finances, home life, family, health, leisure, or anything else you wish to add.

CHAPTER FIVE

GETTING OFF THE HAMSTER WHEEL

Why do hamsters run around and around in circles on that wheel anyway? Our minds are very similar, meaning we have repetitive thoughts over and over that scurry around on that proverbial wheel. We just can't seem to get off the wheel once we're on a roll. It becomes more like a habit and a compulsion, rather than actually trying to sort something out in our minds. It's a bit like the mother who thinks that by worrying consistently, she somehow averts any fears of her children coming into harm. Is it about having some sort of control? Is that what we get out of repeating our thoughts? Is it possible that somehow a solution will come to us if we think about or worry about the problem long enough? For some of us, we just like the misery that it brings us; it gives us some drama to enact. For others, it is such a habit that it has become an automatic reflex of the mind. Like our little hamster, we yearn to rest our minds from their obsessions, for instance, by using meditation.

It's a big word but one with little meaning for some people. Meditation simply means to reflect, contemplate, or ruminate. It isn't as complicated as many would believe. All you're doing is replacing the thoughts of anxiety and fear with love and peace. It doesn't sound like a tall order, but try doing it at the height of your obsession! It's not easy unless you truly stick with it, and then you improve as you go along. We will share some of our techniques with you, things that have worked for us, even if only for a moment. Having that hamster climb off its wheel was a reprieve from all that internal noise—even if that bliss reigned for a split second!

First, find something, anything, that gives you a sense of relaxation without the use of substances (such as drugs, alcohol, and the like). What is it you like to do to ease yourself after the burdens of your day? Do you plan time for yourself and find a place of peace to stop the daily noise? No matter what, meditation is a great way to bring about peace and tranquility to your daily life and your mind. You might be looking to deepen your communication into a more profound spiritual understanding that suits you. Silencing the inner dialogue of misery will improve our thinking as we slow down the processes of thought and remove harmful, repetitive thinking. It boosts the oxygen in our bodies by relaxing our breathing and deepening it, thus slowing down our heart rate and blood pressure for a more relaxed state of being. Who would not want that?

Meditation can be whatever you would like it to be, as long as it calms the mind. We think it can be a phrase, a song, a walk in your favorite place, such as a park. If you have the time, volunteering at a neonatal unit, holding preemies in a rocking chair, is meditative. Perhaps you like to paint, draw, do crafts, knit, sew, woodwork, fish; all of these calm the mind if you allow them to, without judging what you are doing. You might just like to sit and listen to something soothing as you stare into a candle flame. Whatever it is you do, you can see that meditation can take many forms. It doesn't need to be the closing of the eyes and sitting still for even a minute, if you don't want it to be.

All you really want to accomplish is to be able to center your attention, rather than your thoughts. You can use movement of your body as your guide, such as Tai Chi, or nature as a feast for your senses, including flowers, trees, birds, or even water. Wind blowing through the trees can be particularly soothing. Just remember, your mind begs for time off too, so find something you can participate in, which will bring relaxation and replenishment for your mind, body, and soul.

When you bump into things, knock things over, or whack your head on something and hurt yourself, the universe is saying you're lost in your head. In other words, when you're getting lost in an issue, you're getting lost in your mindset. This feeling is almost like watching ourselves go through the motions and not being able to avoid or see when a negative event is going to happen. Often, it is a warning to our minds to be present, instead of drowning in our negative thinking. When you bump yourself and you're not aware of your immediate surroundings, you're not keeping yourself safe—physically and possibly emotionally.

As a result, you're not in the present moment; the screaming monkeys in your head can be distressing. There are some who are constantly in this mode, never aware of what is outside them and too aware of what is going on inside their heads—internal babble that just won't shut up. It is used to having control. When you bump yourself, it can give you more reason to be upset—or it can actually bring you back into the present and allow you to cry out in pain or suffering, so you can release your troubles. However, we can also bring ourselves back into the now by simply doing a grounding meditation. You can use this technique whenever you need to refocus and thus allow yourself to know you're connected to everything, instead of separate. This can be done while standing or sitting, whether you're washing dishes, taking a bathroom break, or having a moment of anxiety or even panic. It really doesn't matter where you are; you can endeavor to bring your mind into the present moment anytime you feel the need.

If sitting, sit comfortably with your back and spine in line, so that your upper body rests upon your pelvis and hips. Alternatively, you may stand with your feet hip-width apart.

Keep your feet flat on the ground, arms and hands resting comfortably (not crossed or folded).

Relax your shoulders.

Stretch your neck and head in order to relax, if required.

Close your eyes to reduce the amount of visual stimuli you take in.

Relax your tummy muscles.

Breathe normally and with rhythm.

Imagine your feet are the roots of a tree, slowly growing downward into the soil.

See your roots growing and reaching into the earth. Imagine the earth rich and brown, filled with goodness.

With each breath, imagine your roots going deeper and deeper, growing strong and thick into the earth.

Your roots now will wrap themselves around a big rock or whatever you imagine as your steadying influence.

See your rock in vivid color. Feel its influence as it steadies you. Once steadied, start to let your branches grow up into the sky.

Grow and reach for the deep-blue sky. It may be night or day, whichever you prefer.

See the constellations in the sky, and the moon, the sun, and clouds floating by in a gentle breeze.

Your branches grow and reach upward.

Once you have finished growing, be aware of what is around your branches. What or who is sitting at the base of your tree? What season is it? What type of tree are you? Do you have leaves? Keep a journal each time you do this meditation, and watch the changes that occur.

If you're not very good at visualizing, you can use a candle to focus on instead. Just don't get lost staring into the flame. Remember to breathe and relax while being aware of your body and surrounding boundaries.

Another technique Spirit taught us for breaking negative cycles was through changing our physical behavior. To get away from all the bad feelings you might have, consider a physical act you may not normally do when a particular situation arises. You might start in some small way, like setting up coloring pencils and books for the kids and then joining in even briefly, or going to the bathroom for a time-out by yourself and combing your hair, making a tea for yourself, or maybe excusing yourself to wash your face and hands. These are just a few ideas you may wish to try.

Additionally, one of the most powerful things we can do for ourselves is redirect our negative and worrisome thought patterns. Start by asking questions such as: *What am I getting out of thinking like this? What are the payoffs that keep me in this cycle?*

You can use these questions whether you're in a mode of self-destruction, victimization, stubbornness, conceit, greed, impatience, self-blame, gossip, manipulation, jealousy, anger, vindictiveness, guilt, hate, perfectionism, or procrastination—or whatever else you're going through at the moment. For example:

MODE: **Self-destruction**

Re-direct and ask yourself what it is you're feeling that makes you want to destroy.

Feeling anger or fear is basically a result of the lack of love, so bring love into yourself by doing something that says, "I love me!" It can be a small act of kindness, like allowing yourself to be loved instead of permitting yourself to destroy your self-esteem and self-worth. The loss of control over loving oneself brings about doubt, feelings of anxiety, fear, and many critical thoughts, including guilt and shame. Part of this questioning is asking yourself, "What am I getting from behaving in a way that is less than honorable to myself?" You may be reinforcing thoughts of being worthless, embodying someone else's opinion—which is a reflection of *their* pain, instead of being the beautiful person you truly are. Why do you want that opinion to be accurate? Because it creates drama for us to play out, and for some it gives a meaning to their lives that serves as a substitute for creating the life they want. Again, we're back to feelings of undeservedness and a lack of love for oneself, rather than setting personal boundaries within ourselves that are nurturing and kind.

The redirect question can be used for all the negative self-talk you use. If you want to dig deeper, you can look up the words, so you can get a feel of what they mean to you, and then look at the antonym. For example, let's look at jealousy—envy, resentment, suspicion, distrust. What do these words conjure up in your mind? Do you see a person, a circumstance or event in your life that represents these words? Now let's look at the antonym, trust—faith, hope, conviction, confidence. With the opposite of jealousy, does anyone come to mind who is related to these words, or is there an event in your life that represents trust? Use that to redirect your energy to a more positive way of thinking, instead of drowning in the negative emotions that only affect your health and your mind. Look at the following affirmations we have used often.

Victimization: I deserve *joy*, not suffering. *Today*, I will do *one* thing that gives me happiness.

Conceit: I am *good enough*. I do *not* need to put down another human being in order to validate myself.

Impatience: I am exactly where I need to be, in this moment and time, as I do not always know or need control over *everything!*

Hate: I do not wish to create hatred in my life. I choose to send loving thoughts to those who harmed me, realizing that they lost themselves somewhere along the way by creating pain for another. Then I will use the power of thought to visualize that which brings me love and joy, whatever that might be for me.

Guilt: I do not need to punish myself. I will learn to move forward and release myself from the shame of my guilt, which is my self-imposed prison.

Vindictiveness: I only wish good things for others and myself, regardless if I think they or I deserve such things.

Gossip: I concern myself with my own being, not with the welfare of others.

Jealousy: I enjoy and love what I have in my life, instead of filling my being with thoughts of lack and not seeing the beauty I possess daily. I bless others and their good fortune.

Perfectionism: I am fucking perfect; live with it! I am unique. There is no one like me in the world, and for that, I realize I am perfect in my own right.

If all else fails, try humor! Try thinking of something extremely funny that made you laugh hysterically. Often, it will trigger other memories of funny moments that will have you smiling and chuckling to yourself. Remember, don't take yourself too seriously. Think of some of your own goofy moments. We can all be silly sometimes, and there's nothing wrong with that. People think we're weird and have told us to our faces! But it usually doesn't stop them from joining in the hilarity. In fact, most of them will say they feel really good in our company. (This is due to raising the "feel-good" hormones responsible for our sense of well-being, whereas living in a constantly negative environment depletes those feel-good hormones.)

If the affirmations above are not worded the way you would say them, word them any way you wish. They aren't carved in stone, nor do they have special powers that they need to be said the way they are written. The special power comes from you and you alone. Say it the way you would like it to be said, and don't worry about it. We all have our own language; what is blue to one may be purple to another. Be yourself.

One other thing to consider: if you aren't in a place to forgive or show love toward someone who has hurt you, it really isn't necessary to feel that way in order for the redirecting message to take effect. You are where you are, and if you cannot see past the event or person, it is most certainly okay to feel that way. Consider it a place to grow from, in whichever way you wish to grow. At the end of the day, your growth is yours, and your pace is yours.

CHAPTER SIX

THE THREE RULES OF LOVE

"The first rule in LOVE is flexibility; the second rule is non-judgment; and third is willingness. These can be switched at any time depending on the event."

—God, 2001

LOVE DOESN'T DISH OUT PAIN. It has a beautiful quality of acceptance and joy for no other reason than who you are. Love *loves you!* When you show someone what love is, you are showing them that they are allowed to have that love too. Even if you are setting boundaries, you are mirroring for them the integrity and dignity of love. Some people believe that in order to be truly loving, one must sacrifice oneself and one's own happiness for another's sake. For some, it is what God asks of us. Love is equated to suffering instead of joy.

Love is about opening our hearts and minds, but not for the sake of allowing another person to harm our well-being. We decided the opening quote regarding love would fit well with the concept of loving oneself. Then we started to ask some questions for clarification.

HELEN: What does God mean by flexibility, willingness, and non-judgment?

JEN/UNIVERSAL SOURCE: Flexibility in mind—remembering that you are all at different stages of development and encouraging others to love oneself, with respect and dignity toward others and sharing that love and knowledge.

Willingness in mind and body to share no matter who they are or what they represent. That is between them and their free will and Creator.

Non-judgment is allowing your fellow men to express their views without judging. It means sharing the knowledge of free will and the power of creation for the benefit of humanity and helping others find love within and in their daily lives. Most people just want to be loved, even if they leave their socks on the floor. You can teach them [understanding] about not purposefully using another human being in a negative way or being careless about another's feelings.

YOU ARE GOD, YOU ARE THE CREATOR, AND YOU ARE THE SPARK! What can you get from God other than yourself? Your TRUE self.

HELEN: I decided it was necessary to question God further as to how these three rules applied to loving oneself and their actual application. Since the book was about self-love, it only made sense to me to use the quote on love given years ago to build a foundation our book would be based upon. I learned something that would change the course of this book.

There are no rules!

This was our e-mail discussion.

From: Jeanette Bishop
Sent: Wednesday, March 08, 2006 8:49 AM
To: Helen Varga
Subject: question please

Hi Hel,

Spirit doesn't understand what you mean by the "Three Rules" - expand on rules????

They say there are no rules.

Just let me know what you would like to see here in that section.

Thanks sweetie

Love Jen

From: Helen Varga
Sent: Tuesday, March 14, 2006 7:18 PM
To: Jeanette Bishop
Subject: question please

Are willingness, non-judgment, and flexibility the three rules in love??

If not, then what are they exactly in terms of love??

That's what I had written down a few years ago during class.

"These are the 3 rules and can be switched depending on the event" –

so can they tell me if I wrote it down wrong or maybe misunderstood??

I don't know if things have changed as far as new info – I know what I wrote down a few years ago, hence where I came up with the idea to begin with.

Hope that helps; let me know if that clarifies or if Spirit thinks I'm nuts – hahaha

Love Hel

Since Spirit said there were no rules, we decided people needed to call them something, hence we will use the term "practices of love" from this point forward. As it turns out, God informed us there are actually more than the three practices originally mentioned.

JEN: One has to remember life and the journey therein is always a work in progress. We are all on a journey, much like children in school. We develop skills as we go, and the terminology changes to match our understanding (at that time). What we believe today may not be what we believe tomorrow or the next day.

CHAPTER SEVEN

THE GUIDELINES TO LOVING YOURSELF

HELEN: PLEASE GIVE US A definition of love and an explanation of love itself.

JEN/UNIVERSAL SOURCE: Love, it is an adjective, it is a noun, it is a verb. Love means to have an irresistible urge to feel an emotion that expresses itself in a positive way. It creates feelings of euphoria, peace, joy, adoration, tenderness, affection, devotion, and passion. These are only some of the actions it creates within a being. Love is also unconditional in its truest form, with no conditions other than being, something man is capable of and has proved through the ages.

Love is also pain, in the sense that we feel pain when separated from love. Hence, we feel pain every day as we separate ourselves from the love source of the Creator. We yearn to be fulfilled, and no amount of "doing" will fill that cup up; only love can fulfill our empty cup within.

Just think of how we feel when we are in love or feel loved by others. Although when you feel you don't deserve love, it is ultimately a destroying force, as you drive love away.

HELEN: Where does love come from, and what is it made of?

JEN/UNIVERSAL SOURCE: Love is an energy; it's a series of electrical impulses that we go through that creates the mood in our brain, such as dopamine or serotonin—all of those feel-good emotions and chemicals in our bodies that give us the sense we're all right.

For example, we connect with another human being and go through a honeymoon period where we're in love, and we enjoy that sensation of looking at a person unconditionally. After a little while, that stage is over, and you only love them conditionally—if they do things for you [you have to see the humor in that] instead of accepting our partner as they are. However, let's back up and state it is often because of how we've created our society. We put these thoughts out there, including how we have to be on our best behavior and do everything the right way the first time we meet someone, because first impressions count. Let's say the person is unconditional in the way they think, breathe, move, their interactions with everyone, including being generous and pleasant; they're inclusive, as opposed to exclusive. We're walking along with them, thinking it's wonderful; then we turn around and get fed up a bit because we might think, "They're not paying enough attention to me. Me! Me! Me!" Emotionally we're around the age of five years old; now we've rejected the sense of love. We've taken the pathway of conditionality and then say, "Oh, I so want to be loved unconditionally." We don't realize we already had it; we didn't realize it was going to be inclusive, as opposed to be exclusive. We're emotionally still quite young.

Let's say we evolve from that and we start to decide that it's okay to love everybody, regardless if they're good, bad, or indifferent.

It's all right to be inclusive and allow the love of our life to move forward and be who they want to be, as well as giving ourselves the very same thing while saying, "That's okay."

Now we've reached a stage of evolution in love that states how LOVE is inclusive and not exclusive. What we're doing is exercising the free will to allow other people to utilize their free will and not be caught up and trapped by the outcome and expectation of what that other person is doing. We also have healthy boundaries. We can say, however, that if we loved totally and completely, there would not be any reason for boundaries.

This is what true love is all about—we value our being, and we value other people's being on a totally inclusive level.

Where does this come from?

That is a deep soul existence to recreate the love that we know that we're capable of giving and receiving in a physical way, in a physical life [which we are]. We're in this physicality, this sack of water in flesh; basically, we're spirit in flesh—whether you believe it or not, it's immaterial, because of all the powers and abilities of creation that you have. Even if you choose to create a loveless life, love will always shine its light upon you and forever be there for you to pick up anytime you wish. It's up to you whether you want to choose that or not. The same goes for loving: when you love on a whole level, what you're doing is helping other people by modeling that role. It's hard to do, because your ego gets in the way and says,

"You deserve that. I wouldn't be going that route if I were you, because they're not going to give you that. You're going to go this route instead."

So where does love come from?

It comes from the universe. It's there at all times. It's an energy that's present always. Just as hatred is there all the time or how the sun shines constantly. The rays are continuously there, but when the world turns, we're in darkness; yet the sun is still there, reflecting off the moon. It will come to you in one form or another.

Love can take many forms. It's very inclusive; it includes everyone, including the martyrs of our world, as well as the dictators of our planet. It's just up to us whether we accept it. So love is a beautiful feeling where we can release all those wonderful electrical impulses within us to create a wonderful existence filled with light, love, and happiness.

Happiness can take many forms. Happiness can just be about being happy to be alive or seeing the sun or a flower; happiness can be about what you're doing. We're all unique individuals, so happiness and love have different meanings for all of us. We cannot label it and say, "That's what love and happiness is."

Love is there all the time for your evolution, for your growth, for you to pick up to utilize whenever you feel like or want to, because you have free will and choice. Love is dependent on what you want to do and whether you value your being or not.

What is the source of happiness?

That depends on the free will and choice of the individual. Most people say they want to be happy. Do they know what happiness is? First, they have to define what they want out of life.

HELEN: Since this book is about loving oneself, why do people hate themselves so much?

JEN/UNIVERSAL SOURCE: *Feeling separate from the Creator, which lies within them, causes people to feel distress. Distress is caused by having a physical body and listening to a physical mind and living in a material world. Lacking fulfillment within the human existence means they have forgotten who they really are and see only what they are in a material sense.*

HELEN: Please explain how and why we feel separate from God.

JEN/UNIVERSAL SOURCE: *You feel separate due to the fact you feel unloved within yourself. You possibly don't love yourself, or others, or are afraid to. You have led yourselves to believe that "God" or the "Creator" is on some level a judge, deeming who is deserving of love and who isn't. However, this is something you have created within your own mind; it gives you the "reason" why you don't feel loved, instead of looking to yourself and your behaviors as to why you don't feel loved. Again, it goes back to creating a loving space and time for oneself.*

HELEN: Where did self-hatred come from?

JEN/UNIVERSAL SOURCE: Your own mind. Whether you believe it or not, you get something out of hating yourself. It ought to help you strive for more peace and harmony; instead, it is used against others, because you think blame, so therefore self-hatred keeps company with your own sense of misery.

Living in a world filled with negative images, which you have created yourselves, weighs down your being.

HELEN: Who teaches us self-hate?

JEN/UNIVERSAL SOURCE: It would be lovely to be able to blame someone else for your self-hate; however, it is you that creates it, so you can rise above it. You want to become self-sufficient. It has taken a millennium, and now it is about un-creating the self-hate in order to be spiritual beings, which in fact you already are. All is about experience, whether you like the experience or not—it is within your power to change it.

HELEN: What do we get from loathing ourselves?

JEN/UNIVERSAL SOURCE: That has already been touched upon—the blaming of others.

HELEN: Why do we hate others, especially those of different cultural origins, religious backgrounds, or sexual preferences?

JEN/UNIVERSAL SOURCE: Everything in the physical world has poles, opposites, if you will. Anything or thinking that you perceive as different is a threat, which means you don't feel good enough in your own right as a human being. So to deal with that, you hate. In fact, that is just another way of loving. You seem to love exclusiveness—religion and sexuality are testaments to that; this way, you can feel safe in the knowledge that you go with the crowd, instead of being unique in your own right.

HELEN: Why were those we trusted and loved the most as youngsters not able to love us unconditionally? What do you do with the pain of this loss, knowing that they will probably never love you unconditionally?

JEN/UNIVERSAL SOURCE: You created this life and every life you are in to become closer to your goal—spirit in flesh. It is all about the experience. When one thinks of some who have used the experience to aid others and bring about understanding, what you are doing is remembering who you really are.

It would depend on each person and how they dealt with their lack of love. No hard answer or black-and-white answer for such a question. It comes back to a sense of belonging. One would need to seek out their sense of belonging and what they love in order to bring about their sense of peace and fulfillment. For each person, there is a route for them to take, and that is the route of love themselves. It would be easy to victimize oneself, so that it would give one the excuse to behave badly or stay in the sense of unlovedness.

HELEN: In the opening of the second chapter, we began with a quote on trust. Can we expand on "seeking within" and how to go about it?

JEN/UNIVERSAL SOURCE: Within a being is the place to begin. For example, if you were to believe everything you read as gospel truth, you would be a robot; same goes for expanding yourself within. Within you is the truth of who you really are. How often is a man taught not to cry, yet he wishes to express his emotions by shedding tears, be that for joy or sadness; he is wishing to express himself by crying. He may fight that later on in life by using anger or frustration to show how he feels, as he has been conditioned not to cry.

If he were to work on his inner beauty to find he really needs to cry and actually allows himself to cry, he might find himself crying lots to begin with, but as he learns to be himself, he would allow himself his moments of shedding tears when he truly needs to. Even if he needed to [cry] lots, there is nothing to say that he can't, as long as he is being truthful to himself.

Therefore, instead of looking to others to dictate who you are, you can seek yourselves by reaching into yourselves and deciding who you are and what you stand for. The truth of the matter is, you grow from whence you started in the first place. Therefore, what you know of yourselves at this present moment may not be you in the future.

HELEN: Here's the big question: how do you love yourself?

JEN/UNIVERSAL SOURCE: Loving yourself is about taking care of yourself in all aspects of life. Simplistic but true.

1. *Ensure your body and mind gets rest from daily living. What message are you sending to your body if you deny yourself rest or healthy food or just peace of mind? It's a great place for negativity to root and deny yourself wellness.*

2. *Ensure your body and mind are fed good and healthy food, with room for little indulgences.*

3. *Don't take yourself so seriously, so much so that you pin yourself into a pigeonhole that says you are anal and rigid. This can take many forms: rigid about having a "good time"; rigid about others; rigid about oneself and what one does.*

4. *Have healthy relationships or at least understand what a healthy relationship is. If you are in pain continually in a relationship, then it isn't healthy. If you require allies to secure your point of view, this also isn't healthy, and you will need to look at your part in that.*

5. *Speak the truth to yourself as best you can.*
6. *Find ways to speak the truth to others without being blunt or hurtful. Just think how you would feel if it happened to you; it's about what you do to another, because you do it to yourself all for the sake of instant gratification.*
7. *Stop martyrdom; sharing is more conducive to a healthy mind and body.*
8. *Stop victimizing yourself or others; it is a negative energy, which spirals into negative behavior.*
9. *Stop bullying others into what you want them to do or say; be big enough to state your own case without needing validation for it. If you were sure of your convictions, you wouldn't need validation in any shape; nor would you need to sound big just to be big. Also, don't condemn another just because their opinion is different from yours. Tolerance is the key and acceptance.*
10. *Allow others their convictions; after all, it is their journey.*
11. *Be supportive of yourself and others when needed.*
12. *Don't judge! That is not your job; once you judge you are saying you are superior to that person, place, or thing.*
13. *It's okay to have an opinion; just don't use it to judge. Your soul knows exactly what you are doing.*
14. *Love yourself enough to steer clear of negativity. If you gossip, you are saying that you don't care what others say about you, which means you don't care if you receive negativity.*
15. *What is settling within your bones? What's deep down within you that you've always wanted to do? You can start small. Feel your way around. Gain confidence. Gain abilities. Nevertheless, just go for it. It's behavior that doesn't harm another human being or behavior that doesn't step over another's boundaries with the use of coercion, manipulation, bullying, victimizing, superiority, inferiority, persecuting, rescuing, untruth, deceit, pain, and suffering at that time or at a later date. It's those things that truly make you happy. Whatever your creative desire that molds you into who you are. Love yourself enough to express yourself at the beginning, and it will evolve into something different as you go along.*

HELEN: How can we let go of our resistance when it comes to loving ourselves?

JEN/UNIVERSAL SOURCE: Resistance is pain and suffering; therefore, it is the condition of the human being due to the way you look at your world and everything in it. The way you look at your world develops when you are young, and your movie inside your head develops into what you have learned over the years, into what you need to fear and what you need to resist. If you feel unloved or unlovable, you will resist forms of love, which are unconditional and will seek love, which causes you to pay for the privilege through your body and your mind. Even if you crave love, you will be unable to accept it because you feel unworthy.

You are beautiful in your own right, and loving yourself for a split second everyday is enough to start that ripple effect in your own lives, in your own being, and with everybody that you meet. Hence, you will end up doing wonderful things for your body and mind, indicating you are ready for more abundance.

Furthermore, we often resist the impulse to love and replace it with the impulse to lash out or be argumentative, rude, or literally protect ourselves from some perceived evil or enemy. We resist a lot of good, for example, the homeless person in the street. We say to ourselves, "I'm not going to give them any money, since they're just going to buy booze and drink it all away anyway—even buy drugs with it." We don't really know that; we go by the common denominator of societal thinking, and we resist our inner beauty, because maybe we truly wanted to help that person. Maybe that compassionate part of us was active at that time, and yet we resisted it. We resist on a daily basis.

We resist so many opportunities in our lives that could be good for us; just look how many people resist quitting smoking and kill themselves slowly with cigarettes. The same applies for alcohol, drugs, and the like. They resist doing good things for themselves because it allows them to have all these addictions or whatever it is that's negative, allowing them to victimize themselves all over again.

We resist the inner beauty we have, because it may appear weak or vulnerable. We could be taken advantage of; it could appear that we have no boundaries. That's part of our resistance.

Why do we resist? It goes back to not feeling good enough.

We have to control; we have to have some amount of power. We have to feel superior in some way, because that makes us feel better and once again in more control of whatever is going on. If a tornado came through your town and hit your house while you were in it, would there be anything you could do to prevent it? There is absolutely nothing you could do. If you had a heart attack because you resisted eating a healthy diet, would there be anything you could do about it? You might think that you're in control, but you're not.

All you can control is how you think and act and what you do to yourself, as well as how you respond to other people. If you're going to resist healthy attitudes, healthy eating, a healthy mind, and a healthy body, then you can expect trouble for yourself—physically, mentally, emotionally, and spiritually. It only stands to reason because of cause and effect. Yet we cannot seem to understand that.

In addition to that, sometimes we resist success because we're afraid of succeeding. We may think more will be expected of us and people will want something more of us. What we don't seem to understand is that once we're successful, we're quite capable of giving more, because we are in a better place to do that. If we are successful spiritually, mentally, emotionally, as well as financially, then we're in a place where we can give more. Of course, the more we give, the more we receive, and that just keeps going and growing.

We resist all of those spiritual attributes because we are afraid. It's such an unknown quantity; we have no idea where it's going to take us, how it's going to take us, and what's going to happen next. If we continue to keep our own frame of reference and keep behaving the way we've always been behaving and the way we've always thought, then we know what to expect. We know what's going to come. It's a bit like saying, "Oh, the cold is going around my workplace. I bet I'm going to get it next week." Of course you are, because you've already created a self-fulfilling prophecy.

If you resist all the time, then actually what you're resisting is your own growth. You stay there because you feel safe; you're in your own comfort zone, and as soon as you're out of that comfort level, it becomes scary. That's why the majority of us resist—we don't want to leave our comfort zone because we don't know what to expect. We have this idea that we should have expectations and outcomes of how everything is going to work, while forgetting that we're dealing with a universe filled with probabilities and with human beings also filled with probabilities as to how they might behave. (There's no telling.) A person can stop on a dime, turn, and change direction; you could trip over them.

Resisting is pointless. The only thing you can do is go with the flow and change; accept that everyone has his or her own opinion and thought processes and their own ability to do certain things. If we have expectations, then we're setting ourselves up for a fall, because that will be the one time when our expectation of another human being falls short. We'll be upset because of it. In fact, you're not upset with them; you're upset with yourself because you set yourself up. That's why we resist.

In many instances when we resist, it's like the two-year-old having the temper tantrum, screaming, "No, I won't! No, I can't." Usually we're resisting love at that particular moment in time. We don't want to admit we need love in order to survive; that we desire to embrace love and succumb to its power. That would mean that we're weak and have no control.

Isn't that what falling in love is all about? Why do you think it's called *falling* in love? You don't step into love or sidestep into it, or for that matter walk backward into it—you fall in love! No matter what you're falling in love with, you give yourself up to it, and it's only when we start recognizing we all have shortcomings that we usually have a problem with love. We start to see things in a different light, instead of accepting what it is we're receiving— something beautiful called love.

We want to control and manipulate it, and that's where we end up resisting. We resist love because we cannot control and manipulate it. If we start doing that, what happens? We lose that thing called love. It doesn't stay. You can try resisting it, but you're going to be very unhappy. That's why many people are unhappy, because they do resist that love. We're not talking about love between a man and a woman, such as sexual love, although that might count as part of it (which is part of another book). What we're talking about here is that honest-to-goodness sensation of being loved for no other reason than for being you.

When we have that kind of love, for some reason, we think we have to reach a goal with it. There is no goal to be in love—you are, or you're not. It's not about where you "sort of" love them. You do or you don't. There's no halfway measure. There isn't a rule of thumb for love—you either love another person, thing, picture, child, animal, scene, tree, or whatever it is, or you just sort of *like* it.

Love is a deep, spiritual connection with a thing, place, moment in time, or human being. You feel connected at that time, so if you ever wonder how you can feel connected to God and the universe, fall in love. When you fall in love, you're open to everything beautiful from that moment on. You have the answers to everything that bothers the human race at that moment in time. You have clarity; you're lucid; you're not lost in any kind of negative thinking (except if you're afraid you're going to lose the love, and then you try to control or manipulate it to suit your needs so you can hang on to it). Forget it! You're going to lose it anyway, whether it's in one, five, twenty, or fifty years.

When you fall in love with something, you're deeply connected to the universe at that moment in time. That's when you need to stay open to that feeling and to that thought; you can recreate that within yourself on a daily basis so that you stop resisting love. You can recreate it within yourself and call back the feeling you had. Force yourself to feel that without pain, knowing that you experienced love—even if it was just for a split second. Then you can recall that and feel much happier on a daily basis. Eventually, love will return to you, because what you're saying is that you deserve love, so it will come back.

CHAPTER EIGHT

THE PRACTICES OF LOVE

Practice 1: Flexibility

HELEN: How can we take the concept of flexibility and apply it to loving ourselves?

JEN/UNIVERSAL SOURCE: The definition of flexibility is to be supple, give, elasticity, limberness.

If you decide not to be flexible in some way or another, toward yourself or others, then you create a vessel that can be shattered. You are that vessel. One is not saying to allow yourself to be abused. However, being flexible with the power of love for yourself and the other person you are dealing with just might result in a spiritual revelation. Ultimately, the choice is yours.

Being flexible with yourself is allowing creativity to blossom, instead of being rigid and noncreative. Being inflexible, you harden your vessel to the possibilities of love and creativity, which only creates negative emotions and feelings, and thus the ego once again protects by sending up walls and feelings of insecurity and fear.

Practice 2: Non-Judgment

HELEN: Please explain how non-judgment applies to loving oneself.

JEN/UNIVERSAL SOURCE: Judgment can send the individual into a spin of pain and suffering when it is applied to oneself in a negative way—admonishing ourselves into believing we don't deserve, we punish ourselves constantly.

The underlying emotion is lack—a lack of love, a lack of support.

Using non-judgment when loving ourselves and others in daily life is a great tool and releases one from the sense of having to judge just because we want to feel superior or having to judge because we want to belong to a certain group.

The more we judge others and ourselves, the more we deflect our own feelings of lack.

Non-judgment can be used in gossiping. For instance, one can say, "I'm glad I don't have to judge that for that person." Each person has his or her own path to walk. Who are we to judge, and what purpose does it have anyway?

Within ourselves, it can be used as a tool to stop the constant barrage of negative thoughts. Why are we judging how we did something? How does that serve what we are doing? For instance, recognizing how we can change something for the better is good; however, judging without a solution is negative.

Practice 3: Willingness

HELEN: Please speak more about willingness and how it applies to loving oneself.

JEN/UNIVERSAL SOURCE: Willingness is the ability to be open to love and experience it. If you don't allow yourself the experience of love within yourself, the inside of your being, be it physical, emotional, or mental, will experience the destruction that accompanies the lack of love. This will reveal itself in many ways in your behavior toward your world and the way you react to your thinking, your emotions, and how you treat your body. Willingness to open yourself to love, so you can experience the peace and joy, instead of pain and suffering, which is part of the resistance to love; willingness to recognize this is part of learning how to let go of the fear and open yourself.

Willingness is the term we use when we are either eager or prepared to look at things or to experience things. If you truly want to be loving toward yourself, you have to be willing to look at the behaviors that actually create unlovingness.

Willingness can take many forms. Are you willing to look at the areas where you're not good to yourself? Are you willing to look at behaviors where you are sabotaging yourself? This is the willingness part of it—being willing enough to actually go through the process and understand why you're not loving yourself as best you possibly can.

Practice 4: Courage

HELEN: What other practices of love are there?

JEN/UNIVERSAL SOURCE: Bravery is having the courage to actually face your demons and know that is all they are—mental demons. Often they are in place since childhood, as opposed to something that you've developed as an adult (unless you've had many negative adult experiences such as drugs or alcohol, where you've done damage to your brain cells). It's to have courage to let those demons go and be true to you and love yourself.

To apply courage, you are going to have to use your willingness and tenacity. You're going to have to be like a pit bull and say to yourself, "I refuse to believe this frame of reference that I have inside of my mind that tells me I'm a piece of shit, because it isn't true."

Practice 5: Relinquishing Control

JEN/UNIVERSAL SOURCE: Relinquishing control means when you've come to a point where emotionally, physically, intellectually, mentally, spiritually, and sexually you can do no more—then, it would seem you have to let go. Often, we let go when we've exhausted every avenue. This does not mean exhausting every avenue isn't the way to go; however, sometimes we need to relinquish our control earlier. Trying to walk a fine line is not always easy, because society says we should be going to the nth degree with all our responsibilities. Often, we don't need to take it to this extreme level. We just have to take a step back and say, "There's really no more I can do at this point."

Sometimes what we need to do is just let go and relinquish control, because when we're dealing with individuals (and there's only six degrees of separation), we find that our need to control everything can be very great. We can really see where we actually want to control too many things, instead of allowing other people to make their own decisions so they can learn through them in order to grow.

If we get overly anxious and we don't relinquish control at the right time, then we actually have more of a chance of negating what it is we're trying to do, as opposed to bringing what we desire forward. We actually cancel the whole thing out, because now it's replaced with a negative energy. Instead, we need to back up a little and state, "I'm falling into a negative pattern here. I need to relinquish control."

We need to give ourselves some breathing space so we can make decisions based on a positive action, as opposed to a negative one. So many of us expect instant gratification, and so we make decisions right on the spot. We just need to relinquish control a little bit and say, "I have some decisions I need to make. Those decisions don't need to be made right this very instant. I can take at least a few minutes just to calm my mind."

Then go to a quiet place, even the bathroom. Do whatever it is you need to do in order to make that decision a healthy and more positive one, based upon being proactive, as opposed to reactive.

As the old saying goes, "Let go, and let God."

How do you do this? State, "I've done everything I can. I am asking for the highest and the best in the universe. It may not be the way I want it, but it'll be the way which is best for everyone concerned." It may be something as simple as getting through traffic. If you state you're willing to relinquish control and let it go, then you know everything is going to be all right. Somewhere in your being, you know this because you can feel it for a split second. Then, of course, you're back in that anxiety mode again.

As an example, think of sitting with a worry stone, a rosary, a prayer, or a mantra. These things may have been developed to distract us from the cycle of worry, which creates negativity. Yet, there is also the underlying idea that if you don't pray enough, God isn't going to hear you. We create God in an image that is more human than divine, and therefore we limit God. Then we wonder why nothing is answered. The reason is because we're self-limiting; we're fulfilling our own negative prophecy through worrying.

We can let go, let God, and then ask for the highest and the best, and allow the universe to work for us instead of looking for instant gratification and wanting the answer immediately. This is one of the very important practices of love—relinquishing control and allowing yourself to be proactive, as opposed to reactive.

Practice 6: Integrity/Honesty/Personal Responsibility

JEN/UNIVERSAL SOURCE: *Integrity is having the ability to keep your mind balanced and see things from all different perspectives. It means not allowing fear, your ego, or even egotistical happiness (i.e., instant gratification), to get in the way. When we talk about integrity and personal responsibility, we're stating to ourselves that we want to discern and think about behaviors as to how we* can change them to be more healthful, so that they are beneficial to others and ourselves. It means being honest and truthful with ourselves.

It's about taking personal responsibility for any thoughts, actions, and words. It doesn't have to be consistent on a daily basis; you don't have to be obsessive about it. Start slow and small; get used to the idea. Get into the mindset of reaping the rewards in your brain regarding decision-making and how good you feel about making them based upon unconditional love for yourself and others. This unconditional love has boundaries because we live in a world of opposites. Personal integrity teaches us to have boundaries and move beyond certain individuals who cause pain and suffering, which we have co-created with them. Start co-creating in a healthier, loving manner. Primarily with yourself, because you cannot change anybody outside of yourself; the only person you can change is you, because you have no control over others.

PART THREE

HEALING YOUR BEING

CHAPTER NINE

HEALING MENTALLY

DOES YOUR BRAIN FEEL LIKE it is in overload? How often do you find yourself so mentally stressed or even mentally fatigued that you cannot even think straight?

Sometimes the stigma attached to mental illness can prevent us from doing what is right for our well-being. We still seem to be in the Dark Ages when it comes to healing mentally. Asylums, psychiatric hospitals, psychiatrists, and the like all seem to invoke a sense of fear in some. Could our minds be the last frontier no one can penetrate? Alternatively, maybe we like to think we are strong mentally and require no assistance there whatsoever.

Yet, more people than ever are turning to the use of antidepressants, as we are flooded with bad news regarding events at home and abroad. How could we not be affected by it? Couple this with home life, work, relationships, health, and finances, and we are in overload. Finding peace of mind isn't always easy to accomplish, but it is achievable if we take small steps to start with. Rate your peace of mind right now on a scale from one to ten, with one being the lowest amount of peace you are encountering and ten being the highest.

What events in your life are affecting your peace of mind? Consequently, what do you have control over right now, and what do you lack control over at this moment? Maybe this could be the time to use daydreaming as a tool. If you have no control over some situation, daydream a positive result, as this might help to alleviate the worrisome mental strain. There will be events and people in our lives we will have no control over that might result in negative outcomes. However, if we can redirect that thought into a positive way of processing it, we may be able to see that there just might be an unseen benefit attached to that thundercloud.

Consequently, if the coping mechanisms you are using are detrimental to you and/or others, it is probably time for you to seek a more balanced and healthier way to deal with mental stress. Once again, this book is not intended to diagnose, prescribe, or replace medical and professional care (physician, psychiatrist, psychologist, therapist, counselor, and the like). If you are experiencing any type of emotional distress, mental health issues, and/or physical problems, we urge you to seek the proper medical and professional aid (advice, care, and/or treatment) you may need in order to heal. There is no shame in seeking or asking for help. All it takes is courage and willingness.

Let's not forget one important part of this equation: if you can swing that pendulum to the most negative aspect of your thinking, then you can swing that pendulum to the most positive aspect of your thinking.

HELEN: Why are there great numbers of people with depression, especially in Western culture, and what does God suggest?

JEN/UNIVERSAL SOURCE: Depression is just another term for seeking fulfillment. Without fulfillment, there is a depressed area in the mind and brain. In the West, you see more of it because of the linking of people by many technologies, and you see it as an illness of the age, whereas we see it as a lack of love for oneself and fellow man. We see it as a lack of motivation toward the loving experience; we see it as a lack of fulfillment in your own lives. Perhaps the choice could be to release oneself from the depressed area of the thinking. Also, one has to take into consideration the toxicity of the mind and the environment and how that plays a part in all aspects of the human experience, not forgetting how the brain releases chemicals, which in turn dictate the body's responses and how one might abuse one's mind and body through toxins like excessive alcohol and drugs.

HELEN: What can people do to feel less anxious and stressed?

JEN/UNIVERSAL SOURCE: Realize you can control the experience in some way, to make it tolerable. Yet, letting go of control can place you in a peaceful situation; much like letting go instead of worrying, since solutions come from a creative place, not from fear. Only you can decide what you need to do. No pat answers will suffice. Perhaps a walk, a good massage to release the muscles from the tension of what the mind has said to do. Then work on the way you think, if it is causing you stress and harm within.

Daily things can include being vigilant in your thinking, remembering to stay within the moment, rerouting your thoughts instead of controlling your thinking, since controlling thinking might set the whole cycle off again. Try for a few moments at a time, and then move to five minutes at a time, remembering that rerouting your thoughts when they have been used to being a wild child will be tiring to start with, and you will feel like giving up. However, the sure way to release stress is to surrender the mind to beautiful thoughts, whatever that means to you.

Neurological Disorders

HELEN: How are mental illnesses created?

JEN/UNIVERSAL SOURCE: It is free will again. The mind is a myriad of impulses and thoughts that show up in behaviors in the brain and the actions of the person. Where is the mind? How does it operate? These are the questions you might want to ask. Mental illness is brought about through toxic emotions you have decided to experience. Intoxication is a powerful thing to experience, whether it is about power over something or someone; it brings you back to that place of invincibility when you were young. You knew *you could create anything, and you did, until your personal society changed that experience for you to have. Therefore, the experience can be positive if you wish it, and the experienced will show the way to the inexperienced if you choose it.*

Change the experience and you change the world and all in it over time. This is evident in the experience you are having now, at this time, no matter where you are or what you are doing. If you look at your world, it is a reflection of what is going on inside of you—pollution, damaged environment, extinction of species, low tolerance levels, power and control issues, war, people killing people, ill health and plagues, famine, obesity, drug abuse, cruelty, and the like.

HELEN: How can you heal them?

JEN/UNIVERSAL SOURCE: Free will and changing the experience. Naturally, it will take time, and not everyone will exert his or her free will at the same time.

HELEN: Can we discuss the rerouting of neural pathways when we change our way of thinking?

JEN/UNIVERSAL SOURCE: The rerouting of neural pathways is not unknown to the world. It is learned behaviors that route the pathways and persistence. Just as, if you wish to stop smoking or drinking, you would have to change your mode of operating and your thinking and thoughts. In effect, rerouting the thinking away from the desire to drink or smoke. Easier said than done, however, accomplishable. The ego is a powerful taskmaster; you can be the owner of it, or it can be the owner of you. Free will. *Your choice.*

You may have been duped into believing your ego is you, it isn't. It is only part of you, and it can be a negative part of you, which leads you to destroying the real you, which is love, or it can be a positive influence for you. Again, back to the opposites we all have within and which we are reaching out to balance. Struggle is evident when the negative energy, which we all have within us, is fighting for power over the domain of the spirit. "Know thyself" is the way to rerouting the negative energies and changing them into positive energies in your lives. If you truly know what you are capable of, then you can master all within, as you won't be in a place of suppression and denial. Then you can master the negative and understand that your free will can bring to you more positive experiences (which are of a proactive nature), rather than reacting in a negative way to your experiences. This is all created by you to release yourself from reacting to experiences as if they were all life-threatening.

HELEN: Explain neurological disorders such as Tourette's, schizophrenia—how do they affect the mind, and is there a way to heal them?

JEN/UNIVERSAL SOURCE: *All neurological disorders such as Tourette's or schizophrenia are the rerouting of neurological networks which are not the norm, as you know it. Impulses fly across the brain at neck-breaking speeds. The question to ask is what can you learn from it? Go deeper into the cell and its components to find the answer to see if the genetic makeup is showing you that there is a pattern in the genetics of the family. The answer is in the genetics, as always, the process of evolution.*

If you look closely enough, you will see the pattern, and you can decipher from that the environmental impacts and free will which created the pattern.

HELEN: Can God explain obsessive-compulsive disorder, its spiritual meaning, and the possibility of overcoming it?

JEN/UNIVERSAL SOURCE: *OCD is a method in which the person functions—a sense of order when no order made sense. Possibly, it is in the genetics or back to the environmental impact and free will, which created the pattern. Again, you are back to the rerouting of neural networks, which originally derailed due to an impact.*

None of these questions has a pat answer, as each individual is different in their own way. If Spirit were to answer in a solid fashion, I would have to question that.

Life isn't simple, yet it is. You are created and Creator and creating, and out of that, you can glean something new, which will always be experienced, as this is what you are here for. Thoughts are an unknown quantity; the only thing known about thoughts is they are living, and they are either positive or negative and have an effect.

HELEN: How much of our phobias, fears, and illnesses are a result of a past life that we've carried over into this life?

JEN/UNIVERSAL SOURCE: There may be some because some have chosen to reuse them in this life. However, it makes perfect sense to have new experiences instead of old ones. That isn't to say that some will take and use some of the old experiences for whatever reason, for example, to retrace steps to a higher purpose or spiritual awareness, or gain insights they were previously unable to glean. However, there are many who wish to try new things and possibly in a different mindset reuse old things with a different life and persona. So in actual fact, they have no bearing on this life; it is just another way to reuse and learn in a different way and have a different experience.

Thoughts and Beliefs

HELEN: Explain a person's thoughts—what are they and where do they come from?

JEN/UNIVERSAL SOURCE: Thoughts are a series of synapses and events that take part through the mind. We use the brain as the electrical current that carries the thoughts through. Thoughts are living things; they are a living electrical impulse that comes from the spiritual being within the being of the body. Take cells and the intelligence within those cells that create a dynamic response to a living environment, for example, your cells' ability to know[the difference] between hot and cold. How do they know that? How does that single skin cell—a nerve receptor underneath it—know to send out a response [an automatic response] that as soon as you put your hand near something that's hot, you pull it away without a conscious thought? The subconscious thought is, "It's hot—move. We're going to destroy ourselves." Within the finger pads, the receptors are not just for heat and cold but also for pressure, pain, and the like; all these are dynamic responses in our cells. That little cell on the fingertip sends out an electrical response saying, "I'm getting too hot. Help me." When we take our hand away, this is the nervous response. We call it nervous, but it's actually an electrical response that responds to the need. Basically, our nervous system is like 911—it's an emergency. Do you want the police, the fire department, or ambulance? What is it you want? Do you need to put out a fire? That's what the nervous system does—it's an emergency 911 unit; it tells us what's going on.

When we are young, our nervous responses are very immature; we have to learn all about this. When we're born, we are in a tiny little body, thrashing about and trying to gain control over our bodies. When we're in spirit [that is, in the spirit world] we float here and there and do whatever because our thought form takes us there. Now here on Earth, we're in a spiritual/physical body. We have to try to utilize our spirit and become spirit in flesh and use our bodies in a constructive manner, in a dynamic way that allows us to get from point A to B; to have a thought from point A to B; to be able to bring food into our mouth and eat it. When we're very young, we have to rely upon the people around us to supply us with our needs. For example, let's take 50 percent of the population (over 3 billion people) who are in a state of dysfunction, meaning they're not living good lives. Now let's backtrack from that and take the form of karma—reincarnation. [Karma and reincarnation are being used in a very loose way and are not to be taken literally; it's just language that we can all understand which states we're coming from one set of living into another level of existing.] We've been residing in spirit, and we decide, "You know what? I haven't experienced living in Guatemala on a rubbish dump, trying to look for food." We decide we want to have that experience, because we've not had that as of yet; we want to know how to grow through that. (We're not aware of that when we're in the physical body, because we have a tendency to forget.) The reason we forget is that we'd probably say, "Oh my God, I'm three months old! I don't want to be here." That may perhaps sound weird; however, it gives us a place to start. We'll just use that terminology for the time being because that creates a picture in your mind.

Since our mother cannot provide for us, by the time we're three years old, we're picking through garbage. Our life has presented us with a number of obstacles to overcome. Using Maslow's triangle in psychology—which states we need to find food and water, have shelter, be nurtured, achieve self-esteem and self-fulfillment—we can then ask if we are going to find all of these experiences in this situation. We can say probably not, but maybe we will. There's the challenge right there.

We've made a conscious decision in spirit to come into this world; now we start sending out the thought processes. We send out the thoughts of, "Oh my God, if I have to climb up to the top of that garbage pile, I might fall through something, and maybe the rubbish will fall on me and I'll never be found again." There's a fear.

We've all experienced where we've self-actualized our self-fulfilling prophecies. For example, at its simplest form, how often do we state that others have a cold and we'll end up getting it as well? Thus, we talk ourselves into the prophecy. So where does that come from? It comes from sending that thought out there which we truly believe is going to happen. When we convey that thought and presume it to be true, it's a desire. Not because we want it to happen, but because it's become a heartfelt response we think is going to occur—and therefore it does. Hence, the self-fulfilling prophecy.

We're going to go back to our example. Now, let's say the three-year-old gets trapped under a rubbish mound but is found. Out of that, an emergency response team finds and takes the child to a place where they get medical assistance. From that comes a good thing. Why? It's back to the network. We have networked with many people that decided to reincarnate with us at the same time (meaning on that same thought level, not on a chronological or numerical level). For example, a group of souls in the world of spirit decide through communicating, "I'll go back twenty years before you, because I'll be the person who'll pull you out of that garbage." Thought-wise and experience-wise, they've all interconnected and said, "I'll reincarnate here, but I'll come work here, and I'll pull you out of there."

A connection is made.

A teacher might say, "I'll reincarnate here in London, but I'll choose a teaching post in Guatemala, and I'll connect with you then." Not all of those thought forms are predestined, per se—although it may seem like it. It will depend on which thought process we decide to take upon that pathway.

By using the three-year-old Guatemalan child as an example, it is hard to believe you would make a conscious decision at that age. However, if you've been raised in an environment where you had to grow up quickly and provide along with your siblings in order for your family to survive, you're going to have a completely different set of thought processes than a child who's been raised in Texas in an affluent family. Each has different thought processes to go through to make different decisions at that age. The Guatemalan child knows he or she has to go up those heaping piles of garbage, pick through them, and then bring something back to sell, in order to make money for the family. The other thought process of that is, they could be frightened by thinking they're going to fall into the rubbish. Another thought process is, "I'm tired, and I want to go play for a little bit." They may go off somewhere and be kidnapped for human-trafficking purposes; they could fall into a sinkhole and never be seen again; or perhaps they could be provided for by an international charity, sent to school, and have all the medical care they so richly deserve. In fact, they have numerous paths they can take as to where they want to go in life. What they choose is based on free will and choice. It is not completely predestined, but it is in many ways, if you look at it in those terms.

At some point, you might play out something that you've decided you're going to do because of the thought processes you put in. It might take one, ten, or fifty years—who knows? That is up to you as to what you decide you're going to do with your life.

Where does that thought come from? Much of it comes from the spiritual aspect of you being spirit in flesh and your actual spirit or soul (it is the same thing really), which is allowing you to make those decisions. Whether they are harmless or not, it is all part of the learning curve as to where you want to go. You can choose. You might say, "I didn't have any choice in the matter." The reality is, you did have an option, whether it is a small or large choice, be it as an adult or child (that concept being hard to accept for some). If we understand this, what we can do with our children is we can teach kids how their decisions will influence their lives.

Let's take an example of a seven-year-old child who kicks another child. He causes another individual harm. He's creating a reactionary process: that other child can either lash back at him or go tell somebody what happened. The seven-year-old will now be punished or receive some sort of consequence for his action. That child has now realized, "If I hurt somebody, there's going to be an outcome for my deeds. There's going to be a ripple effect for my action."

Teaching children at a very young age how to honor themselves and others in a very loving and gentle way, to be more spiritually active in the choices they make, so they can see at their limited capacity of understanding the consequences of their actions, is to help them evolve in their thought processes.

We're going to end up coming full circle.

We are all a bunch of cells that have intelligence that can remember their state. Hence, if you're diseased, then you can recall a healthful state if you get better. The thought processes are already built into every single cell in our body, which is attached by energy to our spiritual beings. This is why we try to seek out that realization—that love—that fulfillment brings. When we feel fulfilled, we're actually feeling loved; we love ourselves and other people. The thought processes come from there.

There's also another aspect to this. When we have a thought, we automatically assume it's our own. Many of us will say that it's our idea, yet someone halfway around the world could have the same thought. Are our thoughts really our own? It's a dichotomy.

What we have to remember is the ripple effect. Often we're not aware that we're noticing all different levels of energy (mental, emotional, physical, spiritual, and even sexual). All things are energy. Just think how you're breathing the air of everyone on the planet and how the energy of that air circulates the globe. We can give them different labels if we want, but the bottom line is that they're energies we're experiencing. Perhaps it might be the tension between people or fear of some sort or even something very positive. It is our choice what to do with it. You could pick up a thought and tell yourself, "They made me do it from halfway across the world with mind control." No, they didn't. It's your choice as to what you do with that thought, but because we're all connected, we all experience everyone's thoughts. No wonder we get so scattered and stressed out from time to time. Hence, some may have not learned how to be their own person with a balanced view; some rely on others to provide them with a viewpoint.

JEN/UNIVERSAL SOURCE: If your level of thinking is on a plane where you're not in a place of crisis or harm and is based upon the best outcome, with the best loving solution that could be made available to anybody, then you may still pick up some negative responses from others. However, that might be an avenue for you to respond to it in order to change.

How many times have we learned of people who have changed the face of society because they picked up on a thought? We can use Gandhi and Mother Teresa as examples of individuals who did extraordinary things based on a thought. You also have people who have done amazing things on the opposite end of the scale, such as Hitler. His thought processes are still around, and millions of individuals are picking up on it by believing and verbally stating that the Holocaust never occurred and millions of lives weren't destroyed. Yet people did die. However, if we take that to a new level of thinking, we can state quite clearly: just as much as we can take a thought form that can damage the human race, that thought form can also bring people together (just as 9/11 did).

We are creating all of this in order to become more creative in a positive way.

That's what we really crave; we don't desire the negative, even though we head in that direction. The path toward the negative only victimizes us and allows us to become martyrs or even persecutors. We're back to that scenario of victim-persecutor-rescuer. What we're actually trying to do is pull ourselves out of that triangle, because it's very unhealthy. However, it is necessary for our evolution to create the power of our thinking in a more holistic manner, for us to be able to live in harmony, fulfillment, and love with the world we're in.

HELEN: How does one's thinking pertain to everyday life?

JEN/UNIVERSAL SOURCE: *It's easy to see by using the example of waking up in the morning that if we haven't had a good night's sleep, then we wake up cranky. That will affect the rest of our day until something occurs to change our mood, which will make us feel better. That's our thinking—that's not just our body saying we're tired. It's our mind, which states how fatigued we are—the brain. We get foggy. We might be grumpy and counter in a less-than-desirable way, just as someone says, "Do you know where …?" while we retort back, "How do I know where it is?" We end up reacting instead of being proactive.*

Reaction involves responding to a circumstance or event negatively. It's a response, but it's an uncontrolled, not-thought-out response, based on our need for instant gratification. *Proaction* occurs when we think about what we're going to do and how we're going to respond.

We live in a society that expects instant gratification. We have a headache, so we take a pill; we're tired, so we eat a chocolate bar for instant energy; wanting to get high, we reach for drugs, alcohol, and the like. We're looking for instant gratification to lift our thoughts into a more fulfilling state, so we can feel better. What we don't understand, generally speaking, is that we tend to look for things that raise our thinking, so we don't feel bad. Some people thrive on feeling bad or being a victim, because they get a spark of energy from that in itself. However, we normally don't wish to behave in that manner. Often, what we're doing is looking for instant gratification for what we're thinking at that time. We might say to ourselves that maybe we need a donut or coffee to create a high. We're feeding our body stimulants in order to rise up, when we should actually be feeding our *minds* stimulants in order to accomplish that. How do we do that?

What we need to do is control our thoughts.

Repetitive negative thinking drags you down. It's hard work, because you have to keep constantly reminding yourself, "I don't have to think this way." We suggest that in your daily thoughts, you start thinking about more positive outcomes. For instance, if you feel you lack control, the very way to give yourself control is to say, "I don't have any control over this situation, and I don't have any control over others. I only have control over myself, and I'm going to do my best to negotiate my way through it."

This gives you power in itself, because you're not being reactive to a situation.

Furthermore, it's easy to see when you set yourself up to think along a negative tangent, rather than a positive detour. For example, maybe you really want a chocolate bar, and you don't care whether you're thin, healthy, or at your desired weight. As such, you're setting yourself up for self-sabotage by thinking, *I don't care. I'm going to have that chocolate bar anyway.* On the other hand, maybe subconsciously you create some sort of emotional upheaval in your life, to justify reaching for the chocolate you want in the first place, such as calling a certain family member that you know always results in a fight.

If we contemplate how our thoughts pertain to daily life, we can consider what and how we are thinking at that particular moment. You can ask yourself if it is a matter of life or death and worthy of your anxiety. If not, then get rid of it. There's no point in hanging on to things you cannot control. We're so stressed out in our lives that we generate life-and-death scenarios out of mundane "molehill" situations.

When we produce those moments, then we're initiating that adrenaline-producing response called flight or fight, which causes us to have anxious energy. Therefore, what do we reach for when we have nervous energy? Usually, it is some form of instant gratification to bring us back down, such as drugs, alcohol, or food. We are creating this to try to make ourselves feel better, but if we didn't create the anxious energy in the first place, we would feel better.

We can only change these patterns by changing the way we think, and we can start the moment we first wake up in the morning.

For instance, what if we didn't have a good night's sleep and our brain is tired? As soon as you get up in the morning, say to yourself, "I'm still tired, and I'm going to bring myself into my day very gently."

HELEN: How else can you create through your own thoughts?
JEN/UNIVERSAL SOURCE: *Well, you could say to yourself, "I hate my life; I wish I was dead." Eventually, that thought is going to come back and manifest itself, because thoughts are energy. Whether it happens in five, ten, twenty, or more years, it doesn't matter. However, you can say, "I reject negative thoughts and acknowledge I now would like to change the dynamics of my thinking to a more positive way."*

As a result, as soon as you start to alter the dynamics of your thinking, you'll produce a more positive ripple effect. We've all experienced moments in our lives when we've generated something positive. For example, someone comes by with an armful of flowers, and you just happened to be thinking about how you really wanted to buy a bouquet at the florist. You constructed that experience through the power of your thoughts.

This is how you create through your thoughts, because thoughts are living things. They are energy, and they go out into the universe, and somebody out there is a receptacle for those thoughts and co-creates along with you to make that happen.

Let's use the illustration of how the sun shines during the day, and the wish for rain at night occurs, thus creating life in the ground. This is the power of creation. How many times have we said, "I wish it would rain"? Consequently, it then rains. That's the power of creation of your thoughts, sometimes alongside the collective consciousness, meaning other people's thoughts and desires.

You can think of it on many levels; however, we've given a few instances.

What about our beliefs? Beliefs reside within your being on all levels—mentally, emotionally, spiritually, physically, intellectually, and sexually, because you're trying to recreate something all the time. What is it you're trying to recreate? Those negative, repetitive thoughts you have daily, instead of shifting the focus into more positive ways of thinking. However, you can have positive beliefs that will bring positive results, just as negative beliefs will bring negative outcomes. This applies to all parts of your life.

HELEN: How do you change those negative beliefs?

JEN/UNIVERSAL SOURCE: The way to rid those negative beliefs is to admit that you have them and do something about it. There are many ways to change your belief system, but you have to be really determined to want to do that.

State to yourself, "I don't want the guilt and shame. I have nothing to feel guilty or ashamed about. It's okay that I'm this way, because the universe [God, Creator, life force, or whatever you believe it to be in your heart] made me this way, and I'm okay just the way I am."

As long as you're not harming yourself or others.

At the end of the day, if you are harming yourself or others, it's creating another ripple effect for change.

(We, Jeanette and Helen, are not condoning harm; it's back to free will and choice and taking personal responsibility for your decisions.)

HELEN: Can we talk about the ego—how it came about, why we have it, and what do we do with it now?

JEN/UNIVERSAL SOURCE: Ego is part of the mind and your personalities. It was created at the same time as you, thousands of years ago. It is directly related to your senses, keeping you from danger, sending signals to pay attention to. When man was first created, it was a necessary part of living. Man evolved; the ego was part of man when necessary. Man's thinking took on a new wave of thought processes as man developed villages, worked out how to become farmers and make their experience more positive, for the sake of continuing the race.

In order for the race to continue, it was necessary for the mind to develop further and develop new skills. This is attributed to learning, which is no different from the modern day.

Our personalities can be balanced or unbalanced, perhaps a little of both, and that can change in any given situation. The same applies to early man. If you have enough negative experiences, you can begin to believe from an early age that your world is unsafe. However, your fears might be unfounded, and you may be subjected to obsessive thinking from a young age.

Obsessive thinking is easy to see. Do you continually find something to be negative about? It would be a bit like moving from one drama to the next in your mind.

Say you had a problem with a parent one day, and all the memories of pain and angst flooded back. Perhaps you need that memory to remind you that your world isn't safe. Your ego will, in turn, remind you of that and continue the cycle of fear within. Okay, so tomorrow turns out to be a great day, no real fears; you think you are fine, and the world looks great again. At the end of the day, you are tired and weary. You go over your day and find yourself obsessing around a comment made; within minutes, if not seconds, you are back in the cycle, as it triggered a response of fear again. Before you know it, you haven't slept all night, wondering, projecting your fantasy of possibly getting back at that person one way or another.

You might even blame God for this mishap, or Spirit, or whatever higher power you believe in. However, that has happened in your ego, and its need to provide safety has kicked the event into a threatening situation in your mind.

It doesn't know the difference between reality and illusion; only you can decide that with your thinking.

Like a small child, the ego needs to feel safe. That is why man has an ego.

HELEN: Many books talk about the ego, including various philosophies. Some say you have to overcome it, practically kill it off. What do you do with the ego, and how do you live with it?

JEN/UNIVERSAL SOURCE: Spirit had always taught me to try to integrate it a little bit more; try to help it grow up; try to help it understand that we don't need to utilize those kinds of behavioral techniques in order to make it in the everyday world. We can be emotionally, mentally, physically, and spiritually intelligent, but sometimes it is hard, since emotionally we're attached to every outcome, plan, and goal we have. If we release the attachment to everything, then we can see much clearer how the universe is responding to us via other people and what we're co-creating. Sometimes we just have to take a little step back and have a look at the grander picture and say, "If I was to emotionally act out right now, what would happen? Am I going to gain anything long term out of this?"

It's long term that you want to think about, because if you only think about the short term, then the ego is all about instant results. For example, it's a bit like taking an aspirin and the headache is gone within minutes. Of course, nobody wants pain, hence we have pain medication. However, if we create our own pain, then we need to think, "Do I want to get to a state where I have to take the pill and wait ten minutes or more before the pain is going to pass?" Thus, we have to be more proactive in knowing what's going to give us a headache, how it's going to give us a headache, and what we need to do in order to change it from headache to a laugh, a happy thought, or a mutual outcome.

What you suppress or repress will swerve and come out somewhere else. It's a bit like that hot-water pipe. If you block it off, that heat is going to keep building up, the steam will keep building up, and you'll end up with a blowout somewhere.

It's best not to suppress or repress. It might be healthier to look at it from an honest perspective and ask, "How does my ego operate? How do I operate under emotional stress, physical stress, or anything like that? Do I yell and scream? Is that my way of controlling the situation? Do I lash out and hit to try to manipulate, control, and subjugate another human being and/or situation?"

If you're counting on instant results from the ego, the ego will give you an answer to solve a problem, but it's not going to be the long-term answer—it will be short term. Until you have integrated the ego into understanding, it can be a part of the process; we thus need to mature it a little bit.

We can use solutions, as opposed to problem-based thinking. For instance, if we find others being on the defensive or reactive (which makes us want to be reactive in return), we can possibly defuse the situation just by asking in a non-combative tone, "Are you all right? Are you having a bad day?" Showing compassion and empathy may change the dynamics; generally speaking, people just want to be heard. In contrast, if we suspect we may respond to others or events in a less-than-desirable fashion, we can take time away and remove ourselves from the situation. Make sure the individual you are dealing with is aware that it's not about him or her; rather, it's how you're thinking about it and how you want to respond to it. However, if you have reacted to a person or a situation, you can ask yourself, "Did I really need to respond this way?" This will mean replaying in your mind what happened, what resulted, and who said what. If you try this technique, it might mean you'll have to be alert, aware, and awake. Those are three key features of actually desiring to grow and integrate your ego into your being. Sometimes what we have to do is say to ourselves, "Do I really need to think like this? Do I really need to respond to someone else like that? Is it necessary for me to be this way?"

The answer is usually *no*.

It's like the scenario of a child repeatedly asking for a cookie, to which many adults shout, "For God's sake, *nooooo!*" instead of saying, "You know what? I would love to give you a cookie right now, but I really don't want you to spoil your dinner. You can have a nice piece of fruit instead." We're so reactive—it's easier for us to yell than it is to explain. We can say we're tired and don't want to discuss it. The bottom line is you don't want to discuss it because you're afraid. You're frightened you're going to be countered, and you need that control because you're unfulfilled.

You are unfulfilled because you feel unloved.

You feel unloved because you feel disconnected.

You feel disconnected because you do not want to have that love in your life; you want to resist it because you have become accustomed to this way of life. You are used to trying to control; to subjugate; all sorts of negative behaviors like smoking, drinking, not eating healthily, or not exercising.

The bottom line is, we live in a society of instant gratification and instant results, yet we cannot figure out why we feel unhappy and stressed all the time. It's because we create stress on a regular basis via our ego.

We need to integrate the ego and help it become more mature by saying, "Is that my age level? Am I talking from my age group right now, or am I talking like a small child?" The ego will get you into an anxiety-ridden state, so that you react negatively. This will give you justification for feeling the way you feel—bloody awful. However, when you start acting compassionately on a daily basis (or as often as you can), you start to pick up on subtle nuances of your own behavior and how you can validate yourself in a truly wonderful way and reduce the anxiety that so many people feel. For example, if you feel inferior at any given time—threatened by others' success, intelligence, or attractiveness—it's your ego creating it. In order to stop creating that, say to yourself, "I don't need to feel that way right now, since my physical safety is not being threatened. The only thing that is threatening me right now is my own thinking."

HELEN: I always love to delve deeper into the human psyche. I realize it's the ego that wants or needs power and control. However, I'm wondering if there's anything else that Spirit hasn't mentioned?

JEN/UNIVERSAL SOURCE: The difficulty with power and control is we know that we have free will. If we have free will, it's like putting a kid in the candy store and telling them to go for it. The difficulty arises when we feel we're attempting to strive for power and control and we use methods that are haphazard at best. We use intimidation, bullying, or superiority instead of using our spiritual characteristics, rather than those ego characteristics.

It's because we know we can. It's like the bully who bullies the bully; the bully becomes the bullied later in life, and the cycle continues until we personally understand why those things happen.

The power issue is because we are powerful. We have the power of reason, and that reason will depend upon our frame of reference at any moment in time (whether we feel intimidated, happy, sad, or whatever). Whatever frame of reference we're taking into play at that point in time and not using our emotional intelligence or spiritual intelligence, then we're going to seek for higher means of power in order to control things.

That's why we want to control things; it comes from the power aspect. As soon as you have power, you have control to some degree. These two words are interchangeable. We can split hairs on it, but the bottom line is we do it because we can.

Another reason we do it is that it helps us feel better about ourselves. If you think on how thousands of years of genetics have gone on and where we are today (wherever our genetics come from, regardless of where it was) and taking it back to that first cave dweller—he tried to have power and control over his dominion. His dominion may have been a little cave on the side of a hill with a small ledge; yet he wanted to have power and control over it because it was his territory. It becomes a territorial right that has modern-day man stating, "I am the CEO of this company, and what I say goes." That could be true if they have all the information, but that's why they have to rely on other people to do those jobs for them. The power comes from them bringing it to their board of directors. They're not hearing the little person in the mailroom downstairs saying, "I think the CEO should do _____." The CEO catches wind of it, and he makes it his own, because there's no way he's going to lose his position to some employee at the bottom of the totem pole.

We steal power and control; we force power and control; we take power and control.

Again, it's because we can, since we have free will and choice to do that. We can choose to be powerless, or we can choose to be powerful. Swinging the pendulum has created this imbalance that we have of power and control over ourselves, because sometimes that's what we don't have—power and control over ourselves. We run amuck in our own heads and with our habits, without having any power and control over ourselves—emotionally, spiritually, mentally, physically, intellectually, or sexually, because we don't value our beings!

It always comes back to that—valuing the being.

If we valued a being, there might be need for power and control, for instance if a person is truly mentally ill. They may present dangerous or risky behavior toward themselves or others, and then, of course, you have to have power and control over that, because you have to protect them, yourself, and other people. We can go deeper into that and state: if we just changed the way that we think and how we eat and the way we deal with our world—because if we valued our being, we'd be valuing the world we live in and not polluting it—therefore, we wouldn't have difficulties with genetics.

We could take it a step further each time, but it's about the power and control issue and how we need to have control over our own selves and our own thinking and where the creative process begins, as opposed to trying to control and have power over other people.

Superstition and Fear

Superstition and fear serve to keep the mind on the same track. (The same track as superstition and fear.) These two lines of thinking and emotion require feeding, so what better way to keep superstition and fear alive in the mind than to feed them with negative events or perceived events? For example, if I am afraid of someone spilling salt, and if I see a person spilling salt, will this mean I will have bad luck too? Fear is the carrier, and superstition is the notion. The mind is a powerful tool. (Basically, it's about reinventing the wheel.) However, if a person reaches into their mind with true intent to release oneself from fear and superstition, they will train their mind to rise above the fear, thus controlling the carrier, and therefore educating themselves to a higher level of thinking. Some of this type of thinking is passed down from generation to generation and needs no explanation, really; just look at our world and how we fear people we don't understand. However, there is another part to this. We still have fears, which were part of our thinking thousands of years ago, based in lack, fear of attack, and the like.

As the saying goes, "Better the devil you know, as opposed to the devil you don't know." There are many superstitions that will keep you in fear every day, such as don't cross your knives, throw salt over your left shoulder, and so on. The difficulty with them is they insidiously permeate our daily lives, subconsciously planted there by well-meaning family and friends. We actually know better than that. However, we love to make things very complicated, and it gives us something to do and to argue about. When this type of thing prevents you from moving forward and only allows you to move from side to side, then you are probably very unhappy at some level.

Our fear of success and failure are linked to superstition and fear. We fear things because of our lack of love for ourselves and our need to be perfect.

We already are perfect.

Think how some people believe they need to wear a lucky charm in order for something good to happen. We put our faith into inanimate objects (idols) to make something happen, such as a job promotion.

Take the person who gets out of bed and puts his underwear on the wrong way; noticing this, he thinks right away, *Oh my God, is this how my day is going to be?* He's created a superstition through fear by believing that putting underwear on backward or inside out will lead to a bad day. However, you can shift the focus and turn it around by believing such occurrences to be good luck, because they happen to be out of the norm. You could state, "I've just put my boxers on backward. Hey, it's going to be a great day. Something really wonderful is going to happen."

Fear and superstition can take a hold of our lives. It may be living in fear that a black cat will cross our path (even though in Scotland, it's believed to be very good luck). We are attached to superstitions and become fearful of those superstitious beliefs. The superstition about throwing salt over your left shoulder because the devil is watching you causes people to think a good entity watches over their right shoulder, while a bad one is on their left side. In fact, the good and bad are in our thinking. It is our thinking that leads us to believe in superstitions as we engineer their meanings to make them fit. There isn't an inanimate object, entity, or energy out there that makes you believe in the superstition. You choose to do that. It's all about free will and choice again.

It's hard to get away from thinking this way, because you get instant results. Case in point: if you refuse to walk under a ladder and go around it, you say, "See, now my day turned out all right." How do you know that if you *did* go underneath the ladder, you wouldn't still have a good day? We become attached to those beliefs, and we've managed to create results out of them. It's difficult to step away from superstitions because, generally speaking, we believe they make us successes or failures. It's someone believing, "I didn't get the contract because I didn't take my lucky rabbit's foot." Perhaps he or she did or didn't get the contract due to ability, and it turns out to have nothing to do with the foot of a dead (and unlucky) rabbit.

You only have to think of the last time we had a Friday the thirteenth to know that somewhere, your superstition stepped in, and you hoped in a quiet way that nothing bad would happen to you. Sometimes we make that bad thing happen, because we are *creators* in our own right. For example, it's amazing that we would create immense success out of a belief that says we need to close the door three times in order to ensure the energy is good. We do this, and a huge success comes out of this ritual, because we have just won a tremendous business contract worth millions of dollars. We confirm to ourselves, "It's because I opened and closed that door three times." At the end of the day, it's a door with a handle. It's because you believed in the superstition, and you were able to perform as a well-functioning human being and create that success.

If you can create success with a rabbit's foot, lucky penny, closing the door three times, or whatever, then imagine what you'd create if you didn't need inanimate objects or rituals. The universe doesn't understand good, bad, or indifferent, so we need to shift the focus onto our desires, in order to move ahead and away from fear and superstition.

We have become so proficient in creating that we don't always realize we are creating, even when we think negatively. This is also a tool for waking up, and we can use this to our advantage. For example, we can ask questions such as:

Do I want to be afraid every day?

Do I want to create things for myself that may be less than what my true self wants?

Am I at the mercy of the universe?

Well, obviously not. Why, you may ask? Because if we were, we would have had things happen all the time that we didn't want—and we don't. We know on some level that we have the *power, free will, and choice to create.* For example, when someone calls on the phone, and we knew who it was before we answered; when we think a letter is coming, and it does; when a situation turns out the way we thought it would; or when we ask for something, and it comes to us.

We also created superstitions many lifetimes ago, so that we could use them to wake up and to *see beyond the fear* that we create inside our minds. Instead, we still allow it to use us.

Everything is interlaced. Nothing is one-dimensional. When we think about superstition and fear, we can see that we are able to create negative or positive outcomes. Superstition is a tool we use so we can see beyond the very behavior we fear that is going to bring us success or failure. If we can see past that behavior, we go into a realm where we understand on a deeper level that it's actually all of us who are creating the success or failure.

For instance, imagine you're with someone who's extremely superstitious, and you're not. The two of you are sitting in a restaurant, and you spill some salt by accident. The other person becomes very anxious, because he sees the spilled salt on the table and believes that you must throw the spilled salt over your shoulder. He cannot take it anymore and asks, "Aren't you going to throw that over your shoulder?"

Your response to that is, "No, I don't believe in that. Besides, you didn't spill it, so what are you worried about?"

He becomes relieved after hearing this. Upon spending the rest of the day with you, he remains ever watchful, but nothing bad happens. So now, he has a new set of values to look at. He can surmise, "Okay, so if it doesn't materialize for them, and they're the same as me, then how come it keeps happening to me? How come when I don't throw salt over my shoulder, something bad eventually transpires?"

Could it be the person is anxious anyway? No matter the negative event, big or small, it would have taken place whether or not he spilled salt, because of his anxiety.

The question to ask is what is your frame of reference?

If you can look at that, then you are going to see beyond it. You will say to yourself, "Maybe I don't need to do that." However, your fear may take over and tell you, "You'd better do that or else." Your ego is there to keep you safe; it ensures you have food, water, shelter, and protection. Look at it logically: can a few grains of salt actually protect a person? It's sodium chloride—that's all it is. We believe in superstitions because that is what has been handed down to us through the ages. Unfortunately, they have been a part of our society and its cultural fabric, and we are only now breaking free of that. It is important to know that we are in control of our destiny, rather than some entity that has power over all things.

Being able to see beyond the fear is actually taking a leap of faith, a much bigger one than taking a leap of faith with a superstition. What you are saying to yourself is, "Nothing bad happened, and I did walk under the ladder, and I didn't throw salt over my shoulder." If you can stay relaxed in that particular moment, then nothing bad will happen. As soon as we become anxious, we become accident-prone. We are no longer paying attention to what is around us; we are only concentrating on what negative events may transpire. Of course, we create them, and so they happen.

Understanding this, you can use superstition as another steppingstone. How marvelous that we have provided ourselves with all these tools to grow into ourselves!

Chapter Ten

Healing Emotionally

Have you ever thought about what you might require to heal emotionally? Do we know what is ailing us emotionally? It can get very blurry when pain is present in our emotions. We have to ask ourselves what ails us. Is it past hurts haunting our daily lives or possibly current relationships that are dogging our well-being? Even our family life isn't immune to emotional wounds. *As always, we cannot stress enough to seek the professional help you may need in order to heal.*

We found that writing our thoughts down on paper and expanding on them helped somewhat, even if we were in emotional pain while we did this. We found a sense of release and discovery as we opened up our lives and our pain to the written word. You might find it easier to do this with a therapist, so you are supported and nurtured through the process and the different stages you might experience. Choose your professional help wisely, bring a friend, ask questions, get referrals from other professionals, and ensure that the person you choose to help you is non-judgmental. The last thing you need is to be minimized by anyone, layperson or professional.

If you aren't yet able to share and work through your pain, you might be in the near future. Just don't give up on yourself. Whatever state you are in, be kind to yourself throughout. When you are ready, you will know. As with anything worth having, there can be setbacks, but don't be discouraged; believe in yourself.

HELEN: What does God have to say about what people can do to heal from emotional issues such as abandonment, rejection, neglect, or abuse that have caused one's self-love to be diminished or even non-existent?

JEN/UNIVERSAL SOURCE: Releasing oneself from abandonment is the same as releasing oneself from rejection, neglect, and abuse. The person perpetrating the feeling toward you is rejecting himself or herself. They feel bad or even evil, if you will. Your light, love, and joy will only remind them of who they really are, and that is hard for them to accept. Therefore, if you feel abandoned, rejected, neglected, or abused, it will require some change of thinking about yourself by rerouting the negative thoughts that say you deserve the behavior that is being perpetrated toward you.

If you continue to believe you are worthy of abuse, then you will recreate the scenario of abuse for yourself to experience, in order to release yourself from it. Why do that, when you can create a place of well-being within and create a place of well-being in the physical?

If you are a creator, then you can create whatever you wish, so wish for love and happiness, and choose well and wisely. Don't let the ego emotions, which breed negativity, tell you what you deserve. Create the wonderful, and start now.

No one can do this for you. However, having a good counselor will help you find that within you. You may be used to thinking negative thoughts about yourself for so long, you may have forgotten anything loving. However, one usually, if not always, has one event or person or even a pet that says "you are worthy of love and self-love." *Otherwise, you will always seek love from another to salve your pain, and that will never be good enough, because you don't have it within [yourself] in the first place.*

HELEN: Why are so many people turning to drugs, alcohol, gambling, and other forms of addiction?

JEN/UNIVERSAL SOURCE: Fulfillment, joy, ecstasy. The rush you get from being loved; that childlike high of feeling loved drives adults who are in pain into the oblivion of addictions. There they can live their fantasy of being great in one form or another, and while there, for a fleeting moment, their pain is gone. Hence, the addiction to this feeling. Regular life is painful; a drug-induced life for them is a high filled with fantasies of all sorts of feelings. Treat the cause, not the symptom of drug abuse—teach them how to love themselves.

HELEN: How does someone go about finding joy and/or meaning in everyday life?

JEN/UNIVERSAL SOURCE: You need to look within if you cannot find something that brings you joy in some small way. Even if it were only for a moment, it is wonderful that you experienced a moment—better than no moment at all. Start small, and then grow to bigger things as you get more comfortable with being happy. Remember too, your body is making chemicals to ensure you stay the course of sadness, only because you have taught it to. Much like learning to redirect one's thinking about overeating or smoking, the body will resist until you make new chemicals, which create happiness when your thinking tells it to.

If you are used to being sad, it is difficult to change that way of thinking. Just like smoking, it becomes a crutch for life. Don't be afraid of being happy or what others' opinions will be if you are happy. You will usually end up outgrowing situations as you become more loving toward yourself. There is a difference between loving oneself and being selfish. When one is loving to oneself, one wishes to share the emotion of love and joy. Being selfish is only gain for one's own use.

See the glory of life all around you if you can, and start small. Without your world that you created, you would have no experiences at all. So change one experience at a time, be comfortable with that experience, and start a new experience. Experiences are ones that harm no one, including you. This doesn't mean if you decide to leave a relationship that is harmful to you but you know the other person is going to be devastated, you cannot. It means you can! Disabling the behaviors of the abuser helps them love themselves as they hopefully take stock.

Where are you willing to draw the line in your life regarding pain and suffering? Do you wait until you have had enough, or do you stop before then and alter your course with destiny? The choice is yours.

Guilt and Shame

Many people probably think that guilt and shame keep humans on the right track; after all, if a person feels guilty, he or she won't do the shameful act again. If guilt and shame provided the necessary and effective tool to ensure that people wouldn't be maimed, killed, raped, or destroyed, there would be no atrocities on our planet. Therefore, it's obvious that guilt and shame haven't stopped people from committing these acts.

As soon as you're admonished for something and you don't match up (in terms of norms and behaviors) to either a group of people, peers, role models, or those who have power over you (whether it's perceived or real), you then feel guilty. You want to please them, so you feel ashamed and try to suppress that feeling and state, "No, I'm never going to do that again." Just like the alcoholic who states, "I'm never going to drink again. What I did to my wife last night was awful," only to go through that shameful period and feel guilty about the episode, rather than recognizing what the problem is in the first place. Instead, they experience the guilt and shame cycle until they reach the point of blowing up. Repression of most things, including emotions, creates deviation.

When you create repression, you start to deviate. For instance, you might have a little drink now and then and pop a breath mint, thinking you're fine because no one knows. It starts to get greater and greater as the need overpowers you—you weren't caught, and so there's no guilt or shame—until you are caught again. Then you feel guilty and shameful all over again, and the cycle continues.

We need to get a good perspective regarding what our guilt and shame drive us to do. Take, for example, anorexia nervosa. Why are individuals with this disorder compelled not to eat? Why are they punishing themselves? What's the need? That's what we need to find out: *what the need is.* Once you find out what the need is, you can start to heal it. Help someone value him- or herself, and then he or she won't feel devalued and need to feel guilt and shame all the time.

Yes, we need to learn boundaries, and yes, we need to know right from wrong; however, there's no need for the guilt and shame.

HELEN: Please clarify the guilt and shame cycle and the history behind it. How it works, why we do it, and what systematic method we need in order to stop the cycle.

JEN/UNIVERSAL SOURCE: Guilt means responsibility; shame means disgrace or embarrassment. If we look at the meanings, we can see we own the responsibility and the embarrassment of being caught in some act, which has displeased our community, be that our family, village, school, town, or country.

The cycle usually begins when we are young, learning from those we deem to know more of our world and who have power over us. For instance, if the frame of reference of our parents is to believe in certain punishments for "crimes" committed that resemble their life in a different country that was riddled with fear and war, that guilt and shame will be incorporated and reflected in their thinking. It works upon the individual, because the individual wants to be loved and accepted, perhaps to the extent they will seek out a similar experience, either to expand their knowledge and move out of the cycle or to implode themselves into a cycle of pain and suffering.

Looking at this, it is easy to see why we have victim, persecutor, and rescuer; all are required when in the cycle of guilt and shame. To step away from the cycle is to announce to those in the triangle of guilt and shame they too aren't worthy of love (in their eyes); however, stepping away is proclaiming yourself as the teacher and the student of "higher" learning. Excuse the pun.

It isn't easy to liberate oneself from the guilt and shame cycle. Your bodies are built to hardwire themselves through exposure and experience. To change the guilt and shame behavior and to change the chemical reactions of thinking and behavior in the body again means step-by-step working on awareness of your thinking and letting it go. It's relinquishing control on how your thinking wants to control and get its fix, so to speak.

Again, a good therapist would take you through the steps of understanding how you have bought into this way of thinking, and how your own frame of reference will set you up for [having] experiences relating to guilt and shame.

The first step is to be aware you feel this way, whether it is with your family, friends, or workplace environment. Understanding and being perceptive to the events reaching out and pulling you into the cycle will bring about awareness in your being. Anxiety may play a part in the learning process, however, take yourself back to mindfulness of being relaxed and aware that you are only trying to liberate yourself and grow into a more peaceful and balanced person.

Seek to be attentive of your body, as it learns to release less-damaging chemicals as the brain reroutes its thinking modus operandi in a more peaceful direction.

Forgiveness

Pain begets pain, until we're willing to move away from pain. Forgiveness is about releasing the pain and suffering you have experienced, either at your own hands or someone else's; perhaps you had no control, or maybe you did have control and continued to allow it to happen. Only when you are willing to release the pain and suffering while stating, "I don't want to hang on to this anymore. I want to move forward" is forgiveness possible. Is the intent there to love the other human being and yourself enough to let it all go? This can be the difficult part—letting go.

HELEN: Is it okay not to forgive?

JEN/UNIVERSAL SOURCE: *When is it okay not to forgive? What is it that you are forgiving? Perhaps it is yourself you are attempting to forgive for* *allowing yourself to experience pain and suffering. In the end, it is all about experiences you have had. Even if the experience is a dreadful one, it shows you what you don't want, and it shows you how you don't want to behave toward others. Is holding on to the lack of forgiveness allowing you to hold on to the pain? Only you can decide if it is okay for you not to forgive. Conceivably, it gives you a springboard to direct your energies into providing good to the world you live in. For example, the mom who lost her child in a drunken-driving accident may channel her energies into advocating counseling for alcoholics. If the problem of forgiving is causing you suffering, then perhaps this is a signal for you to redirect your thoughts.*

HELEN: Say you actually want to forgive. What would be a systematic process?

JEN/UNIVERSAL SOURCE: What does "forgive" mean? Pardon, exonerate, excuse, let off are some of the meanings. This being said, is it about excusing, or is it about learning to understand why another reacts? Add this to seeing the essence within the person. If we can keep in mind that we all have our own frames of reference by which we live our lives (whether happy or cruel), then perhaps changing the way we think and how we respond to events or cultures which are different from our own, will we start to understand the history behind every event and how it came to pass to have an effect on the people and how fear got in the way and started the reaction which led to the event which laid the foundation for future behaviors. The way to forgive this is to realize we all want something, and that something is to be loved. Some of us know how to reach love in a caring way, and others only know extreme and uncaring ways of control and manipulation. Keeping your boundaries intact and seeing that everyone has their own journey is a start to distinguish the way forward and what to leave behind. Use the event as an experience to utilize further boundaries in which you care for yourself and others in a loving way.

It's also to understand the part you played in it. Whether you were the enabler and you didn't see it at the time because you were vulnerable and you allowed things to happen to you, or you were the instigator—poking, prodding, and manipulating—either by behavior, silence, or talking. We all have our ways of manipulating; nobody is immune from this kind of behavior. Understanding how you do it, in order to survive any kind of experience that comes your way—that is the key. Much like being plagued with anxiety, we control our environment and people to keep our world "safe."

Once you understand your behavior, say to yourself, "I can see how I created that. I can see how I finished this and made it better or worse." Once you've got that down, then you can start to look at it and not feel guilty and shameful about it, because you were acting upon impulse at the particular moment in time. You're only doing the best you can with the tools that you have at any particular moment. When you want to change something and forgive someone, you have to look at those things and say, "I understand my behavior, and I know probably more will come to me as I go along. Now I need to look at the other person and say, 'Okay, I see why they reacted the way they did toward me. I can see why they behaved the way they did, because of their past experiences, their childhood, who they've been with, or what shaped their ideals and belief systems.'"

HELEN: How can we heal and love others as well as ourselves?

JEN/UNIVERSAL SOURCE: You can love yourself primarily. If you cannot do that, love another for who they are, instead of wanting to criticize them or speak unkindly of them. When you do that, you are loving yourself enough not to be caught in that trap of hate and suffering. The ego can be a powerful drug, inasmuch as you can allow yourself the freedom to hate and cause suffering to others, and unfortunately you are only hurting yourself, as you are connected to the person you are hurting.

HELEN: How can we love others even when they've done wrong to us?

JEN/UNIVERSAL SOURCE: If one can remember that when someone does harm or wrong us, they are reacting. What is the cause of this reaction? Is it their own inner struggles, their own inner painful experiences? Perhaps they are affected by toxic events in their own lives, which cause their reactions.

How to love this through is difficult but can be done. Thinking on this, if we can see the essence and understand in a perfect world, none of us would behave in certain ways that cause harm to others. Maybe we need to understand that our world is filled with harmful thoughts, which lead to harmful events. To love someone after they have committed an atrocity is to say, "Who knows what was in their minds at that time and what lack they had when they felt the need to harm others?"

We all want to be punitive, and certainly, consequences are probably the way to moderate and change behaviors. However, if we are more spiritual and share, we may find many people are in pain in some form or other.

It is difficult to love others, because you place conditions upon that love by saying, "I'll love them because …" instead of, "I'll love them as they are." At the end of the day, it is about attempting to love somebody for who they are, rather than placing conditions on them, without losing sight of maintaining your boundaries in the process.

For example, having unconditional love for your children, regardless of what they do or may have done (drugs, robbery, or murder); if you can still love them because you see the essence of their love within them, and you still feel that love, then you are actually loving yourself. Of course, this does not mean you are condoning what they might have done. You are actually stating you see them, not the event. You are condemning the actions they have committed.

Loving somebody else allows you to feel that love, even if it is just for a moment. A moment of loving is better than no moment at all. The old saying reminds us, "Better to have loved and lost than never to have loved at all." If you have never loved, then somewhere inside of you, something dies, because we are meant to love each other. If you can love someone else, even just for an instant, it's better than nothing, because in that space of time, they're reflecting you, and you are mirroring them. That's contact—the connection of love. We're all connected on a spiritual level, because we're all part of the Source. Ultimately, the other person is you, and you are them. By loving another person, you are actually telling the universe that you deserve love, at whatever level that may be (love with conditions or love without limitations, as well as everything in between), even if you do not love yourself.

CHAPTER ELEVEN

HEALING PHYSICALLY

Your body hears everything. It isn't a silent observer in your life.

When you feel emotional pain, your body feels it too; when you feel mental anguish, your body feels it too; when you are in a spiritual crisis, your body is there with you, experiencing whatever loss you have encountered. All those trillions of cells have their own intelligence; otherwise, you would have a toe growing out of a cut on your finger!

Every cell in your body knows what to do and how to do it. If you send the body signals that it is not doing the right things to be well, it may let you know in a hurry. Alternatively, it may take years of pain and suffering for it to manifest in your cells. It might start with simple headaches or aches and pains; past injuries might act up; you may be plagued with fatigue or even disease.

Creating health has to be a global activity. Our toxic planet is just a direct reflection of our bodies and our own self-hatred. Until we control the self-imposed destruction of our planet, our bodies will suffer at our own hands. How can we be healthy if we do not have a healthy Earth to live on? We have to take care of our microcosm (our bodies) and our macrocosm (our world).

Healing your mental and emotional body by caring enough about loving yourself gives the physical body a break from the destructive beliefs and feelings you have about yourself. When you care enough about your body, mind, and soul, you will automatically care about the world you live in. It then becomes possible to say to ourselves, "I am the world, and the world is me. Every action of destruction affects my equilibrium, my physical body, my mental health, and my emotional health."

Maybe we don't have the "old" diseases, like diphtheria, for instance, but we are clever; we have invented/discovered some new ones: hepatitis A-Z, HIV, AIDS. (Here the words "invented" and "discovered" refer to viruses and bacteria that lay dormant and can surface due to "raping" of the land and upsetting the equilibrium of the earth and the human population, this is all discovery, much the same as we discover we have an illness.)

Take a close look at how you take care of your body. Do you tell it you deserve to be sick? Do you think derogatory things about yourself and berate yourself on a daily basis? This only harms those beautiful cells within our being that make up our heart, lungs, kidneys, liver, brain, blood, bones, and skin. For every disease process, there is a mental, emotional, or spiritual cause—there always is. Therefore, if we keep thinking those berating, negative thoughts, which often lead to negative physical behaviors, we will keep manifesting all of those emotions inside of us that toxify our cells.

We don't advocate anything other than the well-being of your mind, body, and soul. Once again, this book is not intended to diagnose, prescribe, or replace medical and professional care (physician, psychiatrist, psychologist, therapist, counselor, and the like). If you are experiencing any type of emotional distress, mental health issues, and/or physical problems, we urge you to seek the proper medical and professional aid (advice, care, and/or treatment) you may need in order to heal. Seeking the medical advice that is right for you is of great importance, for your mind, your body, and your spiritual health. This means it's all right if you feel you need a nose job to make you feel more comfortable in your own skin. However, if you get $150,000 worth of surgery and you are still unhappy, you might want to look at that. Remember: although everything you do to your appearance is an external event (which is rooted in our thinking and emotions), if you do not see the beauty internally, then nothing you do will be of any use to you, *until* you learn to love yourself instead of the illusion you see.

How can you love the physical aspect of your being? Spirit answered some questions regarding this in general terms, because each of us is unique in our own right and has our own journey.

HELEN: Why do we create toxic substances to abuse our bodies, such as tobacco, alcohol, and drugs?

JEN/UNIVERSAL SOURCE: *Your physical world is an amazing place. It is filled with so many things, negative and positive. The creation of these things is for you to reject or keep, as you will. Your free will allows you to do what you will* *and understand your ability to create. If you choose to create substances that will alter your being, then you have discovered what you don't want. Your world is filled with opposites for you to discover; this is your creation. Negative experiences only show you how deep your positive experiences can be and vice-versa.*

You could not do that, say, on the moon or Jupiter. There is only one place you could experience this at this time, and that is your planet, filled with amazing life forms and energy forces.

HELEN: Does environmental pollution actually harm our physical well-being, or can our mental beliefs overcome these toxins?

JEN/UNIVERSAL SOURCE: If you aren't healthy in your mind, then your mind tells your body you are weakened against things. So then, what do you think would happen? One person can smoke for fifty years and have nothing wrong with them because they truly believed that. What is more polluted than smoking? Your mind. Of course, this ought not be confused with it's okay to smoke, or it's okay to pollute, because it isn't. Why would you want to overcome pollution, as opposed to cleaning your planet? Surely it is more conducive to clean your planet for the sake of all life forms.

HELEN: Why are we seeing more cases of diabetes, stroke, and heart disease, as well as cancers, ADHD, autism, Alzheimer's, and AIDS?

JEN/UNIVERSAL SOURCE: Diabetes—simply put, not enough joy in one's life, so you choose to fill yourself up with food, or you may not be able to digest the joy. Genetically speaking, you are reaping the sins of the forefathers; it is the free will of the past that is affecting life now.

Stroke and heart disease—not enough love and not using the mind to create wonderful experiences which harm no one, including oneself.

Cancers—the eating up of flesh; rogue cells multiplying at enormous rates; speeding up of the mind's ability to create negativity. Speaking non-truth, and non-love toward oneself.

ADHD—the brain's ability to think fast on its feet. However, it is derailed by society's need to control by exercising power over a person who has the ability to think and move quickly. It is about not using the perceived problem as a tool for creation. Toxins in our air, food, water, feelings, thoughts, and emotions wreak havoc on the unborn child who has decided to come into this world to experience and teach about free will and use of [it] therein.

Autism—in a world full of illusions, you have a problem with this? An autistic child, no matter how he or she is perceived, is a beautiful child nonetheless.

Alzheimer's—the mind's ability to release itself from the task of daily living. No longer able to deal with the challenge of life, the mind retreats to a safe haven of illusions and memories, eventually retreats, and cuts off life itself. Questions to ask here would be if the person has had enough of life. Has the person followed others and not their own dreams? Has the person been bullied into submission one too many times?

AIDS—difficulty with your sexuality. If you believe your sexuality is a bad thing, then you will reap the rewards of your thinking. Free will once again. If you are irresponsible about your sexuality and do not consider your own well-being, as well as that of the partners you are encountering, you will create with your free will dynamic situations that will create havoc on many levels of your being.

Behind all instances of health, be it physical, mental, or emotional, there [lies] a myriad of thought processes that enhance or derail good health.

It is as simple as that, and yet complicated, inasmuch as you need to have courage to face your fears and rid yourself of them so you can live a happy and fulfilled life.

HELEN: Sorry, but can you please explain what you mean by "irresponsible about your sexuality"?

JEN/UNIVERSAL SOURCE: Being irresponsible with your sexuality is about how you treat your sexuality and the partner you are experiencing your sexuality with, knowing what diseases are out there and how they are transmitted. Is it not time that the choice ought to be for pro-health, as opposed to thinking it will never happen to you or you will never get sick? This is a great way to think, but only if you truly believe it and know it. There are many in the world that aren't there yet, and still they perform sexual actions, knowing they might infect someone with disease. We as a race are irresponsible with our views on sexuality, keeping the old ways of destruction and prejudice toward others.

HELEN: Stem cell research—will it help us or hinder us?

JEN/UNIVERSAL SOURCE: If everything comes from Spirit first, then one has to ask the question, how do you do this without harming? *It is back to genetics and how they operate within a being and what can be aided by this.*

HELEN: Is aging a necessary physical process or just a mental process, or both?

JEN/UNIVERSAL SOURCE: The fact that you wish to have a pat answer tells all. There are no pat answers to any question, due to the amount of creativity one has at his or her fingertips.

The mental ability of the human being is huge. The only thing that prevents the person from seeing how huge the mind is is lack of understanding about how you create.

The process of aging is a normal process for you. You have come to expect to age, due to many factors you have in your daily lives. Therefore, if you expect to age, then your mindset is of aging, so you create aging.

The cellular structures of your bodies are programmed to create life. If it were not so, you would not renew your cells constantly. However, if your mind sends the message to the cells' intelligence to hold on to negative traits, then that will enhance the cells' ability to destruct, or age, as you put it. In addition, there are conditions in the physical world, which are created and are being created to enhance that level of thinking.

HELEN: How much of old age and disease are a part of keeping nature in balance, as opposed to how much of disease and death are avoidable?

JEN/UNIVERSAL SOURCE: It isn't measured in quantifiable portions, once again, more to be viewed as evolvement. Much as a disease will kill the host in order to live—what it is saying is you *are* killing yourself in order to live. *It's a dichotomy, but true.*

How often is it said, "What goes around comes around"? Why you don't believe that to be true for yourself and yet can believe that to be true of others goes back to the superiority of being set against a backdrop of human beings who, in one's mind, are lesser than you. All can be prevented through the power of thought and resetting the nature of the mind into a power of creating positive in one's life.

You have created an explosion of population to experience sharing.

HELEN: What percentage of illness and disease is created in this lifetime, as opposed to past lives, what some call paying a karmic debt?

JEN/UNIVERSAL SOURCE: It would be easy to lay the fault at the feet of a person's past lives. However, if we look at that with the power of creation, we can see that the person has chosen certain things to happen at strategic points in his or her lifespan. When you decide to reincarnate, you have choices (as always) as to who you would like to be, what life you want to have, and where you want to be. All is part of the process of experiencing. The more you experience, the more experienced you become, and you have free will and choice of what you do with that information. If we are to become spirit in flesh, we need to experience all that encompasses that, in order to evolve.

Therefore, you create everything you want to create, here and now, for the **soul** *purpose of experience, if you will excuse the pun. How can one know what one wants if one doesn't experience it? However, one can change the experience by altering the thought processes in creating new and more acceptable experiences. For example, if you are not happy, change the reaction to the unhappiness to change the experience, or just change the experience.*

HELEN: How can we heal physical ailments in our bodies? Why do some individuals heal, while others do not?

JEN/UNIVERSAL SOURCE: Healing comes from within; it is a creation, again, from the mind. Fear is the mainstay of non-healing. Some will heal because they have tapped into their power of creation within their thoughts, and they bring that to the table for others to see. In effect, they are teachers to you. Others may decide that they wish to take off their physical body and become spirit again. Again, it is free will that allows you to create what you will.

HELEN: Is positive thinking enough? If it is enough, then what is the difference between those who think positively and are still not well, as opposed to positive thinkers who are healthy?

JEN/UNIVERSAL SOURCE: Positive thinking can lead to repetitive behavior, which can help an individual to heal. Free will is the difference. The one who is still not well may have decided to take off the physical body and keep the mind positive. However, there may be some who are great actors in showing the world they are positive, yet in the privacy of their minds, they are in pain and wish to return their physical body for a refund into spirit once again.

HELEN: How do spontaneous healings and remissions occur, and why do they happen to some and not to others?

JEN/UNIVERSAL SOURCE: This has already been discussed—free will. You have free will, the greatest gift ever given. You are free will embodied. There are some who wish to take off their physical body and return to spirit and some who have a teaching post to go to.

HELEN: Are there any affirmations or thoughts to use in order to keep the body healthy?

JEN/UNIVERSAL SOURCE: How can one keep a body healthy if one doesn't understand the power of creation? You have created healthy lifestyles; however, one has to create healthy thinking. Obsessions are part of that creation of unhealthy thinking. When we say "you," we mean the population, past and present.

HELEN: Explain spiritual healing and how individuals can use it to help themselves.

JEN/UNIVERSAL SOURCE: Spiritual healing is a force of true love. True love heals all. If a person is recognized by himself or herself as being love embodied, then the spiritual healing that takes place filters into the body. This resonates truth in the cells' intelligence and vibrates balance, which can only rid the cell of its memory of pain until the cell recalls it again. Healing takes many forms. The person may wish to use free will and return to spirit but be healed in the mind and released of pain and suffering, or the person may wish to use free will and create well-being in the body, as well as to continue their journey.

Body Image

HELEN: How can people love their physical body and appearance despite society's standards for youth and beauty?

JEN/UNIVERSAL SOURCE: The physical world is reclaiming its truth to be who they are. However, if one isn't in a loving place in their minds, they will still seek perfection, as they see it, for their physical bodies. It is a learning curve yet again in free will. Your bodies are, as they say, temples, filled with intelligence, love, and free will, to do whatever its driver wants (i.e., you). As you think, so your body will be. It bows to your will and whatever you create. Thus, seeking youth, be youthful; seeking beauty, look to see your own individual beauty. If you were all to look the same, there would be no need for physical attraction. Each of you has your own programming within your intelligence, which says you have free will to enjoy your lives and your bodies. This is the experience of life, and you can use your free will to embrace your beauty, or you can embrace the power of another by allowing yourself to be ruled by the opinion of others and how they define you in terms of youth and beauty.

HELEN: Why do people get bulimia or anorexia?

JEN/UNIVERSAL SOURCE: Lack of love and the need to be loved. Not recognizing you are beautiful in your own right. However, if you don't want to live, the bottom line is you won't.

You are brainwashed, and cruelly so, into believing you are not good enough the way you are. Once this belief is ensconced in your thinking, you effectively have brainwashed yourself into destroying your temple. The positive in this is that as far as you can take that feeling of negativity, swing that the other way into positivity and you quickly see how far you could reach! Again, it is back to free will and the experience. You can control your world with food. Imagine what you could do with other things if you can do this much with so little! The thought is inspiring—anorexics and bulimics could help starving people of the world; they intimately know what starvation is all about. Perhaps this is why they do it.

You have so much, and there are many with so little.

Is it the mirror of what you ignore in your world?

HELEN: Could you further expand on "bulimics and anorexics could help starving people of the world" for us?

JEN/UNIVERSAL SOURCE: If you think about someone who starves himself or herself, obviously they're starving emotionally, physically, and mentally. People in third-world countries go through the exact same thing—all those different realms, planes—those layers we have as human beings. Bulimics gorge till they throw it up; they could help people too, because there are people who are eating whatever they can get their hands on and literally throwing up because they're making themselves sick. "I deserve the food, I don't deserve the food. I will get fat. I better get rid of it so I don't. I can at least eat until I don't want to anymore, then I can throw it up so I don't grow."

It is a direct reflection again. These are mental illnesses that people have when they have those kinds of conditions. They could help people in third-world countries by actually going there and experiencing it for real, because for them, not to eat or to throw up is a choice. That's the difference—it's a choice that they make. Even though that choice is compelled or driven, it is a choice they make.

HELEN: Sorry, but it sounds like the people in third-world countries would be helping those here, and I'm asking what God meant by anorexics and bulimics helping them and in what way?

JEN/UNIVERSAL SOURCE: If they were to go over to the third world, they're going to see that their way of life is not a choice, and everything we do in the West is—whether you're anorexic, bulimic, or obese. It's all about choice, but they could actually end up helping them over there, because it would be a wake-up call, spiritually speaking, of course. Their lives would be made worthy once again, and they could recognize that because they have this wonderful gift of freedom—of free will to choose whether they eat today or not—they could put that to good use. They could help those in third-world countries by soldiering on for them, by helping them in getting the aid that they need.

If we look at anorexia, bulimia, and obesity, it's a cry for help. What people suffering from these ailments don't recognize is they have free will and choice, but then again, they do recognize that, because they utilize it to control the only thing they have control over: what they put in their mouth. Compelling, driven—yes, absolutely—it's the only thing you have any control over at that time when you feel your world is out of control, so that's why you need to control things. When they have that much choice about their control, think about what they could teach other people about having free will and choice and control and to utilize that in a healthy way.

Third-world country people are no different. They try to control, but do they really have any control over their governments or whether they get aid?

Hence, they could champion marvelous causes in third-world countries, such as teaching them about control and how to manifest for themselves in a positive way, as opposed to a negative way. Collectively help them gain control—as villages, small towns, and eventually huge communities—then they would have a voice.

Chapter Twelve

Healing Spiritually

Until you have your own spiritual experience, no one can tell you or show you what is true or not. It is a subjective experience, not an objective one.

Healing spiritually simply means having a well-balanced relationship with your own life force and inner self. What does that mean exactly? It can mean anything you want it to mean—your divinity, your soul, your sense of godliness—whatever you perceive that to be. Even if you are an atheist or agnostic, your spiritual self is the life force, living a physical life, yet has an intuitive, instinctive, and insightful side to it that is innate, regardless of religious belief.

A life force is the vigor by which life gives birth to itself every day. A life force is anything that is living; it propels itself through life by being able to hunt and gather food for itself. It has a circulatory system and a nervous system; it is an invertebrate or a vertebrate—carnivorous, omnivorous, or herbivorous. It just means a living thing; anything that is living is a life force. The water and trees are life forces. Each of us is a life force; so are insects, birds, animals, even rocks, because they hold minute microbes and life forms in them. Our whole planet is a life force. When something is living and breathing in some form, as everything does on our planet, it has a life force—and it has a right to be valued.

However, to value something as wonderful as our Earth and our own beings might be a huge responsibility for some. It might mean we cannot do what we want to do, and we will need to change our perspective from dog-eat-dog to "do you want to share my bowl?"

It's not easy when you have been led to believe you are entitled, instead of understanding that we all deserve good things, which we can create ourselves!

Even if you think this is a bunch of hooey, you still have to have a relationship based on love with others and your world. Whether it is your spouse or partner, your family, your pets, you develop love through your interaction with them. Sometimes we have relationships that defy reasoning; this is the innate part of us that loves regardless of circumstance, which is sometimes mystical and revered by us. We would certainly classify this as spiritual, as it knows no boundaries to its love. *Spiritual* often conjures up thoughts of something holy, based on some sort of divinity. This is not necessarily true. *Holy* just means something sacred, in this case, something sacred to *you*. It could be the divinity of Christ, the sacredness of Buddha, or the Hindu deities. Whatever is sacred to *you!*

Healing yourself spiritually involves making sure your own sacredness is kept intact and has a place to grow within you.

If you allow others, society, or the media to take away your relationship with yourself and cause self-doubt, this can damage your innate intuitiveness. It can take away the instinct for happy living and the insights into life and relationships you have with people and animals. Your world may be distorted to the point where you might be unable to tell what is good for you and what is not.

Our spiritual being is very important to who we are. Tapping into our spirituality doesn't require any belief at all, other than knowing you are a creator, creative, and constantly creating.

To heal this part of us is to go into that space of peace and calm every day, to allow the inner voice to speak—the inner voice that keeps us in our place of happiness and sees all things as a stepping stone to greater understanding. Going into this space can take many roads; your map is your feelings. Usually the inner voice is one we have all heard but not always recognized. Commit to memory how it feels when you are aware of hearing the voice within. It can be a sensation of peace in the mind where creative thinking takes place; it can be through meditation, or it might be that place where you are on autopilot. Being aware of when the stillness is within and the sense of peace and tranquility has emerged will help you find the inner voice.

The inner voice is that "knowing" that you have inside of what is right and wrong for you. The difficulty occurs when we cover that up with our sense of what we want—not necessarily what we desire in a wholesome way, but what we may desire in a negative way for ourselves. We can be all about controlling our environment and everything around us. The only difficulty that comes from this is that we often attempt to control the world around us and the people in it, including ourselves, in order to achieve an outcome we think we want. Often, what we think we want is not what we really need at all; it's not even healthy for us. Want only creates more emptiness, because when you want something and you actually get it, then of course it's not fulfilling for you, because you're going to want something else. It just creates more emptiness within. Want actually creates a lack of fulfillment within your being, because you're seeking outside of yourself, as opposed to within yourself.

Seeking wholeness inside yourself is not easy, because your body is filled with toxins and triggers in your cells that state, "You really want that chocolate bar because you're hungry." What you probably need is a piece of fruit or a drink of water. No one is saying you cannot have the chocolate bar, but if you continually turn to those of kinds of things, then obviously you're creating desire within your cells because you've made your cells toxic. In order to hear that inner voice, sometimes you have to stop doing toxic things to yourself. It can be once a month, once a year—it doesn't matter how many times you do it; it doesn't have to be every second or every day. It can be whenever you feel powerful enough in your own right that you can carry it through. We sometimes do things and push ourselves forward, but we let ourselves down in the end. Emotionally, we're not ready to take responsibility for our being.

For those who want to know how to move out of the realm where one is consistently toxifying body and mind, you have to choose your moment. Just imagine that your ego is a little kid, and listen to what it's saying. Is it stamping its feet while yelling that it wants chocolate, or is it having a hissy fit and telling you that you deserve several glasses of wine so you can let loose because you've had a hard week?

No one is saying you don't deserve these things. However, there is no need to victimize yourself into that process; maybe a relaxing evening, a massage, or reading a book to quiet your body down would work just as well.

We need to calm anxiety down. Exercising, walking, yoga, deep breathing, meditation, eating fruits and vegetables, and drinking water all give our cells the energy and the spiritual, physical, and emotional nutrition to allow them to settle down and release their intelligence to us. It's not a quick fix. We have to take responsibility for our bodies. You have free will and choice as to what you do with your body, and what you choose to do will determine whether you will hear the inner voice or not.

Our spiritual being knows what is right for us and communicates with us daily. Often only in moments of knowing are we aware of this. Knowing happens when we are in a place of openness, peace, and quiet. Limit your thinking, and you will create a cutoff point to that inner spirit that only wants the best for you. In fact, it is you!

Reaction to the opinions of society only generates inner conflict. However, action based on spiritual wellness initiates joy and a belief in joy that is yours. Action with spirituality is understanding that you are whole and complete every single day, even though you might not believe that right now. Your spirituality has no knowledge of anything to do with unlovedness.

Unlovedness is a condition of our world, and there are many contributing factors: family, school, media, multinational companies, religion, and politics. All have opinions of who they think you ought to be. We realize that society requires rules for the sake of order, however, when the rules mess with our psychological well-being and our spiritual health, it becomes a dis-ease.

This is our society's disease: the lack of commitment to our spiritual well-being, thus restraining the spiritual growth of each individual and the freedom to practice our spiritual lives. There is always someone willing to shoot down our desire to be abundant in every way. The common notion is that spirituality has to be performed in lack—meaning we ought to have a begging bowl and a loincloth in order to be spiritual, even holy! This, too, is born out of some religious fanaticism, which dictates that we should not have any kind of physical successes, because somehow God and money just do not mix. Renouncing material wealth and the body's physical pleasures, such as sex, equates to godliness. However, this says we cannot achieve spiritual success because we are not divine enough, spiritual enough, even "good" enough to reach the goal of being spiritual—or not committed enough in the way someone tells us to be.

Being spiritually healthy means allowing yourself to understand that you are human and you will do things that society views as "a mistake." Spirituality is about growing and understanding, nor is it punishment for trying to grow. It also doesn't mean that if you fall short on the first try, you are a failure and you ought to give up or become resentful and vindictive toward the world.

Its process is simple: just learn from the truth of what your spiritual aspect is telling you, and grow, learn, share, and understand from others. Remember that spiritual growth is about self-discovery and experiences. Hence, there are no bad experiences, just ones that allow us to make the decision whether to repeat it or move onto a new experience. Rule of thumb: if you are hurting yourself, another person, or something else (such as a pet or someone's property) then what you are doing isn't coming from a place of love or spirituality. It is coming from a place of pain and payment for the pain. Plainly put, use the Golden Rule: "Do unto others as you would have done unto you."

Don't allow others to take your self-respect and dignity away; outgrow those who cause you pain and suffering; mingle with people who can actually represent love without pain; be in the company of love as often as you can in any given period. Sometimes something so simple isn't easy to grasp, because we expect it to be more esoteric, complicated, or even out of our reach, somehow thinking it is unattainable. It isn't. Keeping company with individuals who represent pain and suffering coupled with thoughts of unworthiness, which signify *misery,* will keep us away from love and happiness.

Stand up for your right to be loved and loving; speak out against any form of hate and pain; and walk away from detrimental experiences that cause physical pain, mental distress, emotional angst, or a lack of love.

It is your right to have love, to be loved, and to experience self-love. It is through love that we manifest our spirituality.

Spirituality has been defined over the ages as an essence distinct from matter. No wonder we have been lost for so long! We think we are separate from Spirit in this format, but although Spirit is matter, it is not distinct from matter; it is within us and connects us in every way. It is another form of energy, just as we are. It is in a vibration form, meaning that it resonates on another level and yet on our level too, much like plants, animals, water, fish, air, insects, and birds are all matter, just in a different form. Spirit is our form, only it manifests itself in a way we are not used to; we just need to look at light, the sun, the moon, or feel the wind. All of these can give us goose bumps, which inform us that we are experiencing energy from our intuitiveness, which is intangible. With that, we can say that each of us manifests our spirituality in a different form.

Generally, our spirituality will manifest itself when another being is in trouble or needs help or when we manifest love. Spirituality is about love, not about religiosity or belief systems; it is purely about love. However, others will have their own understanding of what spirituality means to them.

Yet, if we can love unconditionally, even if it is for a second, then we have manifested our spirit in flesh. For instance, our heart is torn when we see some poor souls crying after a natural disaster, and as a result, we send out unconditional love, that is us manifesting our spirituality. If thoughts are living things and they send out a ripple effect, then that's powerful in itself. It's like the love we felt after 9/11. It was a horrific event, yet think about the love that poured in because of the catastrophe; we were spiritually manifesting ourselves. It can be the little old woman who takes care of all the cats on the street or the schoolteacher who helps the troubled student—anytime we help with no expectation of a tangible reward, it is spirit manifesting itself. We are manifesting our true being spiritually. We are all connected, so you don't actually own your spirit. We share it with each other.

Often we don't think about an expectation of an outcome, because we're not looking for anything. All we see is a need, and we want to fulfill that need in each other. Spiritually we're manifesting ourselves without even thinking about it. This is how our spirit works within us. It draws us, it molds us, and it shares with us the powerful antidote to hate and suffering: love. There are many who can say they've gone into a bookstore and have been guided to a particular book. We can say it's our spirit guides, but the bottom line is that your inner spirit knows what you need. Your inner spirit is talking, and if you cannot hear it, it's going to guide you and raise little red flags here and there to take you to guideposts. That way, you know you're being led by something unknown to you. This unknown is your own spirit, and often we don't hear it. Some people do hear it all the time. However, we live in a world filled with noise and stimuli, so it is hard to hear, but our spirit isn't stupid. It is very intelligent, and along with the universe (which speaks to us every day) can take us on a wonderful journey. We can manifest our spirit and not even know we're manifesting it. We just know we've done a good deed, and we feel good about that, because we've earned something within ourselves. We've earned the right to respect ourselves, to value our own being, as well as that of others.

What is your form of manifesting your spiritual nature?

It is just being you.

You are your own *stepping stone!*

When you awaken to your journey to remember, you become your own teacher and pupil. You will become your own stepping stone to your ever-hungry spirituality. So celebrate each new journey you take into the unknown and every human being you come across, as they will be your angels in disguise, and *you* will be theirs.

How awesome to think that our spirituality is that synchronized.

PART FOUR

THE HUMAN RACE

CHAPTER THIRTEEN

SUPPRESSION LEADS TO DEVIATION

INTERESTINGLY ENOUGH, WE REFER TO ourselves as the "human race." Are we, in actuality, in a race against others and ourselves, with the goal of producing winners and losers? Since we fight others in war, battle Mother Nature, struggle for power and control, or clash for religious or ethnic supremacy, it seems necessary to delve deeper into this area and ask God some hard-hitting questions.

HELEN: Why do we create wars and weapons of mass destruction that cause harm to humans and the planet? How do we counteract this?

JEN/UNIVERSAL SOURCE: Free will creates all, whether you are a poor farmer in a third-world country or a powerful politician. Because the balance isn't restored, you have a world that is unbalanced in its power. Wars are created through the power of thought, and that thought can influence others in their thinking. It is no different if a person burns the flag of another country; it is hate. If a person hurts another human being who is weaker, it is hate. If a person deliberately starves another human being, it is hate. If a person kills another, it all amounts to the same thing: it is hate of oneself.

Unfortunately, due to the number of powerful people who have and will be in power repeatedly, who dictate to their fellow humans in fear and anger will only reap such things. Such is cause and effect. For instance, dictators such as Hussein, Hitler, and the like all dictated to their fellow humans in fear and anger, where anger is the carrier and fear is the notion instilled into the people, thus subjugating and dehumanizing them. They were to protect and care for their nations and did not, so the result of their ego was their own dehumanization—karma, if you will—cause and effect. It is really a larger picture being painted to show the dehumanizing behaviors we are all capable of; many are quick to anger and lash out to gain control. This, on a grander scale, shows us to be aware of our own behaviors and thought processes which are firmly rooted in negative and superior thinking.

Receiving power is for sharing with the people who put you there, not receiving the power to keep it for oneself. The only benefactor then is oneself. Until you can love each other with the only cause to bring harmony, you will always reap the dictator (within either yourself or those in power), remembering that the reason we are here is to experience and remember who we really are.

HELEN: Why do we want power and control, whether we are a dictator, a corporate CEO, politician, or the average individual?

JEN/UNIVERSAL SOURCE: Competition; competing for supremacy over your own dominion; giving yourself the sought-after prize of being a supreme being.

HELEN: Can we talk about dictators and what someone like Hitler was trying to teach us?

JEN/UNIVERSAL SOURCE: They are teaching us we have choice. You have the choice to be a positive influence in people's lives and your own, or you can choose to receive the power for the gratification of yourself. Hence, they became very powerful; they managed to convince their people by ways of force and fear that they could destroy—which they went on to do. This reinforced the message.

HELEN: Dictators rule with fear, as God has mentioned. What is it they really fear, and what steps do they take to be less fearful? What do they need to do in order to heal?

JEN/UNIVERSAL SOURCE: Separation is the fear—fear of being separated. We can only say to make the choice based in love for humanity and not make the choice based upon hatred for humanity or power over humanity. However, this might be a learning curve for all concerned, and who are we to decide what you need to learn and grow from? That is your choice, as always.

Healing comes from healing oneself of anger, fear, hatred, and any emotion that creates doubt and disconnectedness. Love is the answer to that; healthy loving of one's being and others who share the environment with you.

What is to fear anyway? Mostly you fear yourself, as you all know what you are capable of, be it in a loving manner or a negative manner. When you realize you are capable of many things, you can choose which things you wish to create.

HELEN: Why do we commit acts of violence against one another?

JEN/UNIVERSAL SOURCE: What better way to rid oneself of the mirror of our behavior or our thoughts? You have created a world where life is worthless, so therefore you think it is your right to take life or maim life (i.e., living things). It really shows you how crippled you are in your spiritual life. This is part of you; whether you wish to admit it or not, it matters not. In small ways, you have seen how powerful you are as a spiritual being, no matter how you use that. It must be terrifying for you to understand when your mind is in the physical instead of the spiritual.

HELEN: Why do people kill others because of religious beliefs when religions profess love?

JEN/UNIVERSAL SOURCE: Again, you are talking about the realm of power and needing a more powerful Source than you to take sides with you.

It is the human that decides with their free will that the other person isn't right or that God is on their side, so to speak. Self-worth, a lack thereof, requires a powerful ally to squash the enemy—and that is anyone that thinks differently. Religion is a grouping of people who come together because they believe in the same thing, or so that would seem. However, free will *comes into play again as the person starts to exercise their free will and takes a place of power and control. When that happens, the free will then becomes a need for power. The negative aspect of you will create all sorts of experiences for that power to come to fruition. How often have you said to yourself or another, "I wish I could just …" in anger or rage at someone who has thought differently than you, instead of saying to that person, "Thanks for your opinion, however, I have to think about that, as I don't think that way." Fanaticism is born out of the need for power. Mostly, people have nothing to lose, or so they think when they behave or think in this manner. They believe their God to be an angry God, filled with vengeance, when in fact it is they who are filled with vengeance and anger. Their sense of sharing is centered on greed, as opposed to sharing with their fellow man.*

Perhaps spiritual teachings around free will and the power of creation for the benefit of humankind would be the answer.

HELEN: The world turns its back on people who are encountering genocide, be it the Holocaust or recent events in the former Yugoslavia or Rwanda. Our world is a global village, and yet governments and their people watch from afar, until a massacre seems to spring us into action. Why do we wait and do nothing? What are we trying to learn from this, time and again, because we seem to keep doing it repeatedly?

JEN/UNIVERSAL SOURCE: It is hard for some individuals to rock their boats, to recognize and become enlightened to the fact that their fellow man is capable of many things, including horrific acts of violence. It would mean they might have to do something that would take them out of their comfort zone, and that isn't an easy thing to do.

Simply because we can choose and make the choice to make a difference or we can choose to make the choice to ignore what is happening. We can choose to make a difference in any way we are capable or able to attain, for the sake of humanity, and become tolerant citizens. (I say "tolerant," as it indicates we will all have our own opinions about anything you care to imagine; tolerance indicates a willingness to listen, even if we don't agree.) Or we can choose to ignore whatever is happening—effectively being an ostrich and burying our heads in the sand. For example, do we ignore negativity, or do we expound on the beauty of positivity alongside with understanding why negativity exists? How many times are we being taught the lesson of tolerance? Where does it begin? Is it the home, is it work, is it our relationships, is it in our hometowns, the societies we belong to, our countries, our world? It is everywhere. Not to overwhelm the reader with this but to guide the reader into looking how to make the world better and what each person could do if willing and also possibly witness within themselves when a moment of intolerance is revealing itself to them raising their consciousness.

The global message is that you do this in your own back yard, too—ignore the plight of your fellow man on your own doorstep. Think of the homeless and what they go through—hungry children, men, and women with no prospects of a reasonable life. Your compassion is selective, and this is what you choose. Of course, this is a general statement and not meant to offend anyone who is making a difference in your world. It is back to choice again. Please remember that the laws of cause and effect are always in place.

You are learning about how to make the choice for improvement of spirit into flesh, as opposed to being spirit in flesh only when you think you need to. Creating a better world starts with you, and the spread of that starts with you. You elect governments. You can change the world by raising your voice to be heard by them in order to make change.

Ensure enlightenment is part of the change by raising awareness of the spiritual truth, "Do unto others as you would have done unto you." When you look at that statement and look around the world, it has an impact on your soul. Love rises, but because you live in a physical world, it doesn't always stay.

HELEN: Besides selective compassion, why do we allow others to suffer and go without?

JEN/UNIVERSAL SOURCE: *In the grander scheme of things, the visible isn't all. Learning to be deeply spiritual humans takes sacrifice, if you will. You* *would need to go against all you know, in order to give to others. Therefore, you receive without your inner knowledge of sharing. Therefore, you are thinking there is lack—as above, so below—lack appears as you have created. Perhaps you might say, "It isn't happening here, so why should I give?" You also judge the fellow who has nothing. Or perhaps you might think the neighbor ought to go and get a job. There are many ways of judging which prevent sharing.*

HELEN: Mankind would love to control Mother Nature; can you please explain the reason for the ever-increasing rates of natural disasters?

JEN/UNIVERSAL SOURCE: Your free will to create in your minds the thoughts and actions to destroy. Cause and effect. You cause something—it has an effect. Charge a nuclear test bomb, release its toxins into the air, and displace the surface atmosphere—you have a recipe for a disaster. Simple, really, if one would only look at how great a creator you are.

Yet, you have the ability to create wonderful events too.

HELEN: Why do we continue to pollute and harm our environment?

JEN/UNIVERSAL SOURCE: You continue because you can. How better to self-destruct than to collectively blame each other for the destruction. Collectively speaking, you don't need to take responsibility, because if the person down the road does it, why shouldn't you? So, in effect, collectively speaking, you are destroying each other and your habitation because you can. You have free will. The environment reflects your pain and suffering.

HELEN: Why is our technology surpassing our humanity?

JEN/UNIVERSAL SOURCE: The technology comes from Spirit. What you do with that is your experience. Perhaps all things will be made known in time and the message will become clear. Perhaps the message is already clear to some. If you have people using the technology for negative gain, then out of that will come positive gain. The message or the question is who or what do you desire? Only you can answer that; you have free will.

HELEN: Regarding competition: why do we continue to do it, and where did it come from?

JEN/UNIVERSAL SOURCE: When you decided to have the experience of the physical, you also decided what you wanted to do and create.

So in order to live all those years ago, you would need to compete with your environment to survive. This gave you the impetus to evolve. You no longer need to compete, however, your striving for better and better only aids the evolvement and brings about change, so in actual fact, competition, in a healthy way, is a great thing. It is when you decide to negate your being in order to try and be someone else or validate yourself against another—who is you anyway—it comes out murky and negative. However, the negative pole is the same pole as the positive, so in real terms, you are teaching yourself about the "reality"—which is love and joy—and that fulfillment comes into being when one regards oneself and others in that light.

HELEN: Can we also address the idea of sports and winning or losing? Is it healthy?

JEN/UNIVERSAL SOURCE: Sports is another way of stating that the human race is still top on the evolution ladder. Validation is rewarded by the means of trophies. However, if it becomes murky and negative, then in real terms, once again you are teaching yourself. You are really looking to love yourself and create fulfillment; thus, gaining that by means of what you consider as foul play is only hurting yourself, as the opponent is you anyway. You are connected, whether you like it or not.

HELEN: What about corporations? Are they a good thing, and do consumers really benefit?

JEN/UNIVERSAL SOURCE: Corporations like to validate themselves and what they do. It is a show of validation; the product or the charity donations are greater than others. The great thing is that many do benefit from it in many ways, and the other side is that many suffer from it also. Again, it is back to the experience.

HELEN: Why do we have perfectionism in our world?

JEN/UNIVERSAL SOURCE: You have created perfectionism in your world. You create a product to sell, and with this product, you feed your family (income), until someone else comes along with the same product, with some different feature. Now you need to make something better and make out it will be perfect. Thus, perfectionism is born.

HELEN: What is Spirit's advice on how people can let go of striving to be perfect? How can people feel and know they are perfect in their own right if they don't believe it?

JEN/UNIVERSAL SOURCE: Well, no one can know or feel it if they don't believe it. It has to come from within. Doubt is the enemy, and the mind creates doubt to strengthen your power of creation. How better to get over something, or create something new than by creating an adversary to what you want to create? Then you feel as if you have earned it. Your choice. It also lets you know the opposites and the illusion of such.

HELEN: Often enough, (although not always), those who experience the need of perfectionism have a high level of expectation and expecting the best from themselves, from others, or from a situation. Spirit has often told us not to have expectations, especially of others, because we

have no control over another person. Can we go into further detail about what the difference is between expectations and expecting the best?

JEN/UNIVERSAL SOURCE: Expectations are of a preconceived notion of what you think is and will happen. Expecting the best has no real preconceived notion, other than expecting the best. If you expect the best and put a notion upon that, then you are having expectations. What is best anyway? Moreover, according to whose rule of thumb or frame of reference?

You can *expect the best from the universe; just be careful you do not put* expectations *upon that outcome. Sometimes you won't know what is the best and for whom it would be the best.*

Trying to achieve perfection is an unrealistic goal. If we are all unique, then whose measuring stick are you using to gauge your own level of perfection? You are perfect in your own right as an individual, and if we are all individually perfect, then we all have something to share with one another. That doesn't mean to say we should be unrealistic, because it's not about being perfect; it's about being human. It's having compassion for one another, as well as learning and growing with each other, rather than competing with others or creating negative scenarios that we play out against one another.

Maybe shifting the focus from perfectionism in our world (both inner and outer) to that of potentiality is the answer. We suggest you start with yourself!

Potentiality is in everyone, and therefore we all have the ability to achieve our potential. The difficulty is finding our own potential. For some, reaching their potential is very scary. Do we believe we are worthy of reaching our potential, and do we know what our potential is? For each person, the potential will be different. Your potential lies deep inside of you. Potentiality is the ability to come to full fruition of who you are. If your mindset is at a place where you are feeling hopeless and helpless, then your potentiality is going to be limited until you are able to release yourself from that bondage. Even if you do something small every day, it is a great accomplishment, because you keep directing yourself toward your potentiality. Spiritually speaking, it is what you desire the most that will provide you and those around you immense joy. After all, who would want to reach a potential that would harm or cause destruction in any way?

HELEN: Even if we reach our human potential, many feel inferior to God. How do we let go of this concept of feeling inferior to a higher power? Any specific thoughts or exercises to utilize would help.

JEN/UNIVERSAL SOURCE: Being conditioned to believe in an unseen power that has the capacity to "strike us down," and using what we have created ourselves as the proof of this unseen power is difficult to shake for some. As the saying goes, "The proof is in the pudding." However, if we think about our own power within, we can readily see we have inner depth and influence on our world.

HELEN: I can see, however, that some people will still argue over superiority and inferiority by suggesting that God has authority (superiority) over us simply because we are God's children—despite being made in Its image.

*JEN/UNIVERSAL SOURCE: If perchance God has authority, then why have none of the atrocities been stopped? If He/She/It was truly a parent and had authority, all of this would have stopped by now. It is because you have free will and choice and are **equal** that it hasn't. God, or however you understand a deity, has given you free will and choice, as well as the ability to reason.*

HELEN: God told me directly, "Helen, everyone is your family." How do we stop competing with one another and understand that there is no superiority or inferiority?

JEN/UNIVERSAL SOURCE: A classic example to understand why we are all family is simple: the Earth's air goes around the globe all the time. The air above the United States doesn't just stay over the US borders. The same applies to Australia, Africa, countries in Europe, and the like. All that air everyone breathes in and out circulates the globe. Therefore, what one person breathed in Africa, you are breathing in today, depending on the winds and how it moves around the Earth. The rain that falls out of the sky and then evaporates back into the sky, which then travels around the globe and falls over Africa, is bringing atoms from Germany over to Africa. If we think about it in these terms and that this Earth has been circling in our universe and the air and clouds have been circulating in our universe for millions of years, does that not say something? You are all breathing the exact same air! The oxen in Africa that were butchered for meat also drank the same water that came from the clouds over North America (and vice-versa). How can one be superior if everything is shared?

Moreover, everyone bleeds red, including the animal life. What does that tell you? It tells you that you all have to breathe in the same oxygen in order for blood cells to become red, to carry it through the body, to provide oxygen and nutrients to the body.

Hence, if we cannot value our next-door neighbor, who is four thousand miles away, then where is that going to leave us? (We need to keep in mind that within a global context, there is only six degrees of separation; hence, people everywhere become our global next-door neighbors.) Thus, it leaves us with a deviation policy that states we are not responsible for what happens four thousand miles away.

Yet we may have contributed to it, for instance, by polluting the land, air, and water. People may think that they are only affecting their own society. However, the entire global environment is impacted when people, societies, governments, and corporations choose not to be environmentally responsible. Therefore, we're not actively taking responsibility for our contribution to global catastrophes that happen to people ten thousand miles away; that's the deviation.

Let's go one step further. Take the examples of Rwanda, the Republic of the Congo, or Darfur. If we look at the people who are being hacked and mutilated to death, that energy (those particles) goes into the air. The air circulates the globe, and thus we're breathing in those particles. We're not only polluted as far as the physical Earth is concerned, but we're also polluted mentally, emotionally, intellectually, sexually, and even spiritually. So think about the energy that's released when a person is violently put to death. You cannot stick a light bulb in a socket, switch the light on, and then batter it with a hammer and not expect some sort of result to occur. We're taking it to its simplest form. How can we as human beings attack and maim other beings (human, plant, animal, aquatic, or air life on our planet) without having some sort of effect? There are always repercussions; cause and effect. It's the basic laws of physics. You cannot expect all of these things to happen globally and not release energy that we are aware of, consciously or unconsciously, into our world.

As soon as you take a life, you're unbalancing the Earth. You've plucked someone out from its life source, and there's an empty space now, because that wasn't meant to happen. Yet it did, because we all have free will and choice. However, those who have been casualties of war, genocide, starvation, and massacres, including the teenagers who died in the Columbine High School shooting, also had dreams and lives they wished to realize. People who perpetrate the crime of taking another's life need to feel powerful, so they swing the pendulum to its extreme.

What would make you more powerful than taking a life? Being God.

It's laughable, because you're God all the time. You don't have to do that in order to be God. The Source resides within you at all times; you are that spark of spiritual light.

When you do that, you're actually taking from yourself, because in fact, to do something like that, a little piece of you goes with it, since your energy was attached to that event. You are a whole being, so your entirety is attached to that event—emotionally, physically, intellectually, mentally, and spiritually.

When you do something catastrophic that is going to affect the balance of our nature, this again is the powerfulness of playing God; for example, the person who murders vast numbers of prostitutes and thinks he's doing God's work. Their spark, their light, diminishes when they take another life.

The infinite spark we have within us is a God spark—it is divine in its own right.

HELEN: Earlier in the book, God mentioned the statement "squashing leads to deviation." God used words you could understand as a child. Now, as an adult, during conversations you've used the phrase "suppression leads to deviation"—which is the same thing. I felt this was an important topic to examine, because many in our world wonder why some people may act out in a negative fashion. Can Spirit define what they mean by the statement?

JEN/UNIVERSAL SOURCE: You have developed the nature to suppress, due to societal and parochial views, which have said in the past you are not good enough. Your God isn't good enough if you diverge your beliefs of religion from the majority-ruling religious leaders, your thinking is out of line with the powers that be, and there is no real freedom of speech. So, in your thinking, that [suppression] is a "safe haven" (or so you believe); however, thoughts are living and have energy. Therefore, they move and grow, just like anything else if they gain food; hence the adage "food for thought." To deviate is to channel the energy to another place or position, so you channel your energies that you suppress or hold in to another place. Hence, you often are surprised when you hear of a serial killer who is a quiet person and a nice person in the neighborhood. Their energies of committing pain and suffering upon another were channeled into another place, which they knew was unacceptable to others. Of course, this is an extreme example, however true in most things. Yet, if you were to live life on the notion, "do unto others as you would have done unto you," then possibly there would be no need to suppress your emotions or thoughts.

You can take that a step further and say that if you are a negative person in your mind and your thinking, you will expect *to have deeds done to you that possibly might be negative. Again, it is about changing the way you think and send out those thoughts to the universe.*

HELEN: What forms does energy deviate into?

JEN/UNIVERSAL SOURCE: Because you are all unique, each of you will suppress different things and in different ways. Usually it is love and how you will manifest love and how you will receive love. If you think upon all the levels of energies you possess, it becomes clear how many forms of energy the wandering energy becomes. For instance, emotionally, one might think of hiding one's feelings; mentally, one might believe in ways, which cause pain to others and oneself; sexually, you may behave in a harmful and negative way when generating the bliss of ecstasy with another. There are many ways to stifle energy and cause it to diverge. Each one of you will have developed your own wandering energies, which can evolve into something precious and beautiful, if only you would believe in your essence and joy united with love.

Let's look at sexual deviance, which is a huge subject in itself. If you break it down in its simplest form, sexual deviants are looking for a connection. What kind of connection does sexuality give us? When we have an orgasm, at that fleeting moment, we are totally in love and at one with Spirit and the Earth, because we have this overwhelming sense of bliss and joy. Generally speaking, deviants might be trying to recreate that ecstasy over and over again. Therefore, what this behavior needs are the tools to create ecstasy, or inner joy if you will, without resorting to deviant behavior. Although this is very simplified, there are other circumstances to look at too. Perhaps a child in utero was exposed to toxic substances, which affected the brain and its development, which in turn created a mind that is ill in its thinking and creating. The other factor of deviant behavior is the egotistical "I want to get caught, but I won't get caught" cat-and-mouse-game mentality, which goes back to feelings of superiority.

HELEN: What during a person's childhood is suppressed that eventually creates deviation?

JEN/UNIVERSAL SOURCE: If you suppress any of their natural tendencies that are positive (exploration of their being, their personality of the likes and dislikes) then of course you're going to create a suppression of some sort. What they're going to do is start trying to ignore that aspect of themselves, because they'll consider it bad, unevolved, the wrong path to take, or whatever they understand it as in their young minds. When they suppress that, they push it down or ignore it. If it's a natural tendency anyway, then it's going to explode in them at some point. They're going to experience it on some level, and they'll say derogatory comments or be negative toward that particular profession, such as, "It takes a lot to be a really good actor. There's no money in acting." Or "I didn't want to be a doctor because I might have ended up working twenty-four hours straight and not have a life, and I didn't want that."

Generally speaking, you know when there's a suppression of some sort, because they'll have a negative tendency toward it. They might make statements such as, "I would have loved to have done that, but I couldn't, because I had to do blah, blah, blah." There's always some form of convincing of themselves and others of the reasons why they couldn't do it, but deep down, they might have wanted to do that.

When they come to that kind of understanding (of that suppression), then it might be a driving force propelling them in the opposite direction. Suppression of energy can take many forms; there isn't just one thing that says, "That's suppressed energy." It could take the forms of nervousness, anxieties over various things, inability to make decisions, stubbornness, criticalness, and anything in between. For the individual, it's up to them to ask themselves if they're suppressing any childhood dreams that they would like to see themselves move toward. It doesn't matter if they don't meet that nth degree of where they want it to go, but at least they can experience some of it. Experiencing could mean skydiving, being a pilot, acting, music, dancing, wanting to be a doctor, and the like.

You just have to be creative enough to be able to make it work for you, and that means using your mind and using your creative ability to make things happen for you to create it, so you can have that experience.

HELEN: What has been suppressed that leads to deviant behavior such as ethnic cleansing, child molestation, or ritual killings of children and animals?

JEN/UNIVERSAL SOURCE: Ethnic cleansing is about power and belief in a singular and vengeful right, (as those perpetrating the ethnic cleansing believe they have the right to do so) which isn't open to any other belief. This type of conviction will destroy anything in its path, including people. The suppression here is tolerance and understanding, the ability to compromise and reconcile to the fact that people of the world are all different and they are at different stages of evolvement. Child molestation is the robbing of innocence, power over the innocent, defiling their natural state of joy and love into something subversive and painful. Loss of purity, the need to control purity for one's own selfish gain and gratification and pleasure in a deconstructive manner is the desire of the molester. Ritualistic killing of any kind is, again, power and a belief of faith to bring about change or maintain status quo, appeasing lustful ideals and behaviors, thinking it somehow spiritual and supernatural. It is usurping life itself to gain life or power of some sort, in an attempt to expand the faithful's supremacy. All of the above are a lack of love, lack of understanding and knowledge, an inability to nurture, to love, unrestricted by intolerant principles.

However, when we're harming ourselves (which we do when we partake in that kind of behavior) or another being, the kind of suppression involved is usually anger, which always leads to hatred, which always leads to a lack of self-love and lack of love for the human being and your environment.

HELEN: Why are there more cases of children being abandoned, neglected, sexually abused, and sold into prostitution?

JEN/UNIVERSAL SOURCE: More? Do you see, hear, and think about what has gone on for thousands of years? This isn't a new scenario exploding into the physical world; this is an old scenario, filled with the same pain and suffering. You are still learning about yourselves and still causing the same pain and suffering, because you are not listening to your true selves, that still, small voice which says love is the answer. You still have not risen above your pain and understood that your minds are the key to this dilemma.

HELEN: How can someone who is sitting in jail for murder or rape find a way to love him- or herself? Probably the worst offenders of the modern day are the child molesters. What does Spirit have to say about their behavior? Where does it come from? Why do they do it? Can they be healed? Can the cycle be broken?

JEN/UNIVERSAL SOURCE: First of all, when you perpetrate a crime against humanity, you are perpetrating the crime against yourself. You are connected to the people you hurt. Thus, the approach is to love oneself and understand your own mind as to why it needs to act out in a hurtful way without blaming others. Often, rage is a factor, which is fear unrealized or realized and then acted out, to protect the fear inside. The fear is based on feeling separate from the universe or God, or however you wish to word it, and feeling disconnected from humanity and the positive aspect of living, i.e., a lack of love and fulfillment. The mind is a great thing; it can convince you of the negative and can convince you of the positive. The choice, once again, is yours to decide.

Usually when you commit a crime against a less-powerful person, be that a child or an unsuspecting man or woman, you are saying you want your power back. However, by taking that from another, you are only taking it from yourself once again. Thus, some become serial offenders, because they think that they need more power in order to gain their power back. They are gratified for that moment but seek more, and many are helpless in their compulsion. Ignorance is not bliss; many suffer from the power of ignorance, and many suffer from the power of intelligence, which can be equally damaging if they use it as a weapon, as opposed to a tool to aid humankind and themselves.

Emotionally, there are many walking wounded. Some enact their woundedness, and some suppress it, only to explode later. All things can be healed. However, one has to remember that there are many mitigating circumstances involved. Once again, this isn't a black-and-white situation; it is clouded with many shades of gray. Your environment and societies have much to do with the deprivations (lack of love, lack of integrity, denial of themselves that causes the deviation of behaviors) which go on. Again, it is about choice.

HELEN: Please clarify what you meant by "you are saying you want your power back. However, by taking that from another, you are only taking it from yourself once again. Thus, some become serial offenders because they think that they need more power in order to gain their power back."

JEN/UNIVERSAL SOURCE: In attempting to gain power, a child will assert himself and gain independence over time. Little by little, the parents, teachers, and so on guide the child through the minefield of assertions and self-government. Perhaps, in some ways, offenders need to feel this power repeatedly, because they lose it after every conquest and sexual experience; like obsessions, one has to collect more and more. In their collecting of their sexual experiences, perhaps each time they feel a little less powerful and seek to gain power over and over again.

We have all the attributes of divinity within us, but as soon as someone commits corrupt acts that go against that divinity, a little piece of them is gone. Their infinite spark becomes dimmer and dimmer, until they have to atone for those behaviors to retrieve their spark.

That's what atonement means: at-one-ment. To be at one. It's hard to be at one when you're diminishing your divinity through detrimental acts.

To atone is to admit that you have done something damaging and from a place of reactiveness. We all do it; none of us is immune from being reactive.

At some point, the light within yearns to be brighter than it is. That is why we're always seeking, because we yearn to be brighter. We yearn for that fulfillment of divinity, that peace and joy we can only get through being balanced within ourselves and enjoying life for what it is, such as the creation of our world. That glimmer wants to be brighter. Acts of kindness, compassion, and openness toward oneself and others allow that light to grow stronger each day.

HELEN: Can you please expand on the statement, "Your environment and societies have much to do with the deprivations ..." and what God means by that?

JEN/UNIVERSAL SOURCE: In your environments and societies, there are many pollutants and toxins, not just of the Earth and the abuse of your natural resources, but of the mind and body. Your minds created all and in turn incurred a departure from the subject of love and joyfulness.

HELEN: Spirit said, "Rage is a factor which is fear unrealized, or realized and then acted out to protect the fear inside. The fear is based on feeling separate from the universe or God, or however you wish to word it." Before you tell us it's a mind thing and we have free will, what can we can do to break these cycles of fear—a step-by-step process, so to speak?
JEN/UNIVERSAL SOURCE:

1. *Tell yourself every time: stop fearing!*
2. *Ask yourself, "Am I hurting anyone?" If the answer is no, then go to number 1.*
3. *If the answer is yes, then re-evaluate and ask the question, "Is it a realistic way to continue, can I find another way to move forward, or is this the only way forward?" If the answer is yes, this is the only way forward, go to number 1.*

Truth is the major factor here. If you aren't truthful, then the mission will be tainted with negative thinking, as you will know deep inside that you are deliberately hurting another. If there is no other way, and they are in a place where they are unable to hear reason, stop fearing. It is their journey to travel, and you must continue on your own path. Stop fearing. *There is no easy way, other than reminding yourself on a daily basis there is no reason for fear—unless your life is in danger, of course.*

When you create the same negative scenario each time in your personal lives and in the lives of society, you are showing yourselves how much you need to choose love and joy when you are dealing with problems and situations that require some work.

If you are with persons who are negative, angry, or tyrants, one can look at it and see they are lacking in love and joy. You can decide to move forward and encourage others to move forward in a peaceful way, in effect turning away from fear-based ideas. However, it isn't always that simple; there are no black-and-white answers to anything you have created. If you think of the amount of effort it took to create devastation and war, you must then also recognize you will need effort to un-create it with the power of negotiation and love.

The levels of negative thinking go far beyond what we might think they do.

For all the levels of positive thinking, there lies the same scale of negative thinking.

The power of love is an immense tool to use. If you can imagine the power of unconditional love, you can imagine the power of unconditional hate. All it is is the same thing—hate is love, and love is hate. Hate is the requirement of love, and when someone hates inasmuch as perpetrating a crime of violence—he or she is saying he or she wants love.

Hard to imagine, really, that someone would ask for love in such a way. However, think of them as being only two years old, and think of the tantrum that a two-year-old might have in order to get what they want. An adult goes on the same way when they are filled with the desire to get love at all costs, only they take it to the extreme, and it gives them negative attention, as opposed to positive attention, and they will take what they want.

HELEN: Many will say that individuals like Hitler, Jeffery Dahmer, or Ted Bundy will end up going to hell, to face retribution for the deeds and pain they have caused. What kind of punishment do these types of individuals actually receive?

JEN/UNIVERSAL SOURCE: If we hearken back to punishment, we are saying that "God" or the universe is a judgmental force. If that were true, then there would be judgment here and now, in the present.

If you talk of the laws of cause and effect, then that is a different matter. Everyone is linked to the laws of the universe; no one is absolved from them, simply because it has no emotional tie to anything or anyone. The universe just keeps rolling. So with that, all cause and effect is reaped at some point. The people you speak of will have their own cause and effect to go through if they haven't gone through it already. That is between them and the universe.

Although there is a difference between acts of deliberation and acts of reaction, they all are linked in the ways of cause and effect. However, there is a difference between recognition and enlightenment.

You can recognize the deed which will need a consequence in action (i.e., effect), and enlightenment of such a deed that required a consequence in action.

Enlightenment is a place of knowing, while recognition is only seeing what has happened and not necessarily being enlightened by the deed.

If enlightenment about the deed isn't there, then energies are enacted by the person to bring around enlightenment, time and time again. Repeating scenarios kind of thing ... whereas a scene replays itself until enlightenment is reached.

As far as hell, as you put it, the place they go to is their own choice. Therefore, if they think they are going to hell, then hell it will be, if they choose to see that. If they decide to awaken themselves to the spiritual truth of their own evolvement, then they will choose to see the learning in their choices of their past life, or perhaps they choose to be who they are in order for enlightenment to take place.

CHAPTER FOURTEEN

OUR FUTURE

OUR CHILDREN CAN ONLY LEARN and grow from what they observe.

We say we love our children, yet it's mystifying that we continue to pollute the environment so that the younger generation is left with the damage caused by our choices.

We insist on starting wars, only to have a sniper's bullet kill our child or a land mine rip off their limbs. "Yes," you say, "however, we're fighting to preserve our land, which is our children's inheritance." The dead children from many of these wars throughout the years are very appreciative of your efforts. It is unfortunate they are not around to enjoy their "rightful inheritance."

There is enough food for everyone, yet we allow our children to starve while the war machine creates trillions of dollars of revenue. Are we not telling our children, in essence, that they are of little value to us?

We commit acts of violence toward others, including prejudicial slurs, road rage, or trading blows over must-have items during holiday shopping, all the while wondering why our children are aggressive and lacking in compassion as they act with indifference. We find it difficult to understand why there is hate in the world, while we don't even recognize it in our own hearts and minds.

You say, "It's not my child; it's someone else's."

The children of the world belong to each one of us, regardless of sex, religion, ethnic background, or blood relation. Spirit has taught us—*everyone is your family. We are all connected.*

One day, our children will become adults. We will find ourselves growing older, with the prospect of having them decide our fate. Is it not in our best interest to teach our children love, compassion, and acceptance? If we have taught them disregard for a fellow human being, then what is stopping them from disposing of someone they feel is no longer of any value to society—in other words, you and me? The child who was taught hatred in another country may one day become its dictator and wish to create weapons of devastation and declare war on other countries in order to control the world. Suddenly it is no longer "over there" but in our very own backyard. Does any of this sound familiar?

HELEN: Any specific advice for teens on how to overcome feelings of unworthiness and what they can do to change their thoughts about themselves?

JEN/UNIVERSAL SOURCE: Teens have the difficult prospect of developing and growing through a hormonal war within and learning to move in their ever quickly growing bodies. If their role models are absent emotionally, physically, or both, their task is harder as they feel their way around their world. There are many teens who are struggling with their thoughts and who they are. Spirit's thoughts are, "You are beautiful, filled with so much prospect for the future. Be all you can be, reach for the moon, and don't be afraid to live your dreams. Be kind to yourself and others, and watch your worthiness grow within you every day, no matter what anyone thinks of you or what you think of yourself. You are amazing, you are a miracle, from the day you were born to this day, a miracle."

HELEN: As far as parents are concerned, how do they break this cycle of unlovedness? What can they do to help their children when there is so much peer pressure to deal with, as well as the media? Any thoughts or exercises that parents can pass on to their children would be of great help.

JEN/UNIVERSAL SOURCE: Bring together your family, learn to relax together, learn how to communicate together in a loving way. Listen to the children; they need to speak their truth, instead of mimicking behaviors of peers. There is much expectation of them. Pushed beyond their comfort zone, they need time to adapt and grow with the world. Even though they are capable of so much, allow them to be children, stay close to them. Even when they show they don't want to be close, they need parents to protect them.

HELEN: What can mothers teach their boys so they will grow up to be strong and confident, yet loving and nurturing, not only to themselves but also to others?

JEN/UNIVERSAL SOURCE: Teach children, not just boys, to be open and tolerant. There is no such thing as a boy's job or a girl's job. What is required is expression of feelings and the ability to talk and listen, so boys and girls will learn to hear their partners and their children when they are adults.

Teach children how to be emotionally present and intelligent, how to share, and how to be loving to themselves, as well as others.

HELEN: If we can exemplify self-loathing through actions, deeds, and words, can we then pass on self-hatred to our children through our genes?

JEN/UNIVERSAL SOURCE: Evolution is what it is. The cell can mutate, as you put it, to become a cancer cell, passed on as susceptibility within the genetic code. There it stands to reason self-loathing will appear as a genetic trait. It is understood that nature and nurture play a part in all children, so therefore, behaviors will present themselves as a trait from a parent. Perhaps you might see it as depression, addictions, anxiety, or immune disorders.

JEN: Spirit taught me how to listen to what my teens are saying. Spirit taught me how to look at them and recognize that they're not just trying to make my life difficult. They're trying to find their place. They're trying to see if I truly love them. When they're behaving impulsively, it's hard for them to stop, because they don't have the adult skills to stop it.

Ranting at them doesn't work; talking to them does. For instance, say your kids are using drugs. You could say something like, "I wish you wouldn't do that to your body and mind because you're so beautiful (or handsome). You have so much to offer the world just by being you. It would be so much nicer for the world to get the real you, rather than a drug-altered you, which may lead you to behave in a way that's going to land you in a whole lot of trouble."

You're going to say these things to your kids on a daily basis, even when they say, "Yeah, yeah, I know." These kids still want to hear it from their parents; they still want to know that they're loved, even if they're not as cute as when they were three. What Spirit really wants to see for those who are parenting teens is that we value our own beings enough so that we value our teen's being. Teens are not always in a place where they're making right decisions, and so we have to help them; we cannot just let them fall. It's our belief system in the world that says, "They know the rules. They know the difference between right and wrong." Yet, they also have an impulsive part in their brain that's functioning at a high level right now. It doesn't matter whether they believe it's right, wrong, or indifferent; if that impulsiveness is there, then they're going to act on it. We can talk to them about it and let them know by saying, "You have a part of your brain right now that's really impulsive. It's going to take time to settle down. How about you check in with me? Let's talk about things first, so I know where you're coming from."

If you direct your focus on them, they'll know that you care about them. They'll be more likely to come and talk to you if you don't negate their ideas or their suffering and pain. What's important is that as parents, we have to realize their pain and suffering is real at that time. For instance, many kids are being bullied as teenagers and being forced into things they don't want to do because they're afraid their peer group won't accept them. We cannot ignore what's happening; instead, we have to help them through it. They need us to say to them, "Make the right decision. Don't do something that's going to harm you, now or down the road."

Teens have to be taught to value themselves—physically, emotionally, mentally, and sexually. This means teenagers will experiment with various things—good as well as bad—because through these experiences, they'll mature and grow into adulthood. My tendency is to advise teens to experiment in ways that aren't going to be harmful to their mind or body and look for things that bring joy, whether it's skateboarding, biking, snowboarding, swimming, even knitting or sewing.

Teens are looking for a place to belong because they feel confused. They just need to know that those feelings often are the result of their bodies growing and maturing. The feelings have nothing to do with not being part of the group or anything like that. Parents need to encourage teens to talk to people who can help them and not those who want to control them or who will bully them. The "right person" may be a counselor, their doctor, or an adult they trust, someone who can help them make good, balanced choices. Talk to them about how you are feeling, and don't just shy away from it. Warn them that talking to the teen next to them in class might not be a great idea, because they could be equally confused.

Keep saying all of the above until they get the message—which they will eventually. At least you know you've done your part spiritually, mentally, emotionally, intellectually, and in a balanced way.

Spend time with them. Ask them what they want to do. Even if you do this once a month, you're spending quality time with them. If you're having a hard time gaining control over your life, you need to look at your own life and divide your time among family, work, and tasks. Find the time to go for that massage, a reflexology treatment, sitting by the beach, or whatever it is you need, so you're more capable of dealing with what's going on. We live in an anxiety-ridden world, and if parents are anxious, kids will be anxious.

PART FIVE

FULL CIRCLE

Chapter Fifteen

Giving Yourself Permission to Be Human

No one said it was easy living in this physical world. Each of us has had one or two tribulations to deal with. Where does that leave us? It leaves us with a physical life to live, with all the unseen mental and emotional trials going on inside. It needn't be that way, though.

The more we learn and grow through our dramatic play of life, the more we are at peace with ourselves. Instead of allowing the drama to play us, we play it, controlling our outcomes and day-by-day dramas as best we can. This doesn't mean we all become control freaks by controlling absolutely everything; it just means we can only control ourselves and our responses to our daily lives by taking care of our beings first.

There is no need to be a martyr to life.

Simply put, the truth will set us free; being true to ourselves without harming another takes time to relearn after much pain and suffering. It takes time for those people around us to get used to who we are becoming and not who we have been.

Give yourself permission to live a human life, not a "perfect" life defined by others.

Everything you do is a stepping stone to greater experiences, and hopefully this book is a part of that. In our efforts, we hope we were able to ask questions that made you reflect and ponder.

CHAPTER SIXTEEN

EVOLUTION OF OUR SPIRITUALITY

THE POINT OF EVOLUTION IS to become more whole, more self-sufficient, to thrive, live, and experience. Take, for example, a germ or virus. You can call it mutated, but what it's really doing is evolving, becoming more capable of sustaining its life and procreating while having a productive life. No matter what organism you are, that's the whole point of evolving. Whether it's a germ, virus, human being, bird, plant, or animal—it's all about evolution.

Spiritual evolution is about becoming more in contact with who we really are. We have a deep-seated knowledge of that. It is innate; it is in us and is always there because we're spirit in flesh. We choose to come here into this physicality because it gives us a great medium to be able to evolve, grow, and use the talents that are part of our minds.

Let's talk briefly about the mind.

There's no actual place where the mind is; scientists cannot find the mind. All we know is that it's a bunch of electrical impulses and synapses that fire at random within the brain. We think it's random, but really it's not. The brain is a conductor of electrical energy and impulses. So where do the electrical and energy impulses come from in the first place? We'll clarify that first before going any further.

A human being is made up of all sorts of electrical impulses that travel through the body. How does the body know what to do? It knows because if we go behind that, we have what Deepak Chopra calls "the observer." The observer is the Spirit; the Spirit is the being. If you are ever present when somebody dies, you realize that a short time before physical death, the person is already gone. You can see that when you look at them. They're not there anymore; only the body remains, going through its process of dying. The Spirit leaves—and that is actually the mind.

JEN/UNIVERSAL SOURCE: *Obviously, science cannot back this up, and neither can I. It just is, until we are able to back the observation up with sensitive equipment. We already know when someone dies that he or she loses weight. When they lose weight, we can say it's their breath, but it's not really, because you can weigh someone when they've exhaled, and they still weigh the same. Therefore, it's not the oxygen. You have so many ounces that have already left the body; if you stop breathing, then those ounces are still there, but if you die, those ounces are gone. So what is that which has gone? We cannot measure it; we don't have anything to measure what it is that leaves, other than Kirlian photography, and we don't know how accurate that is either. We have to keep moving forward and evolving, in the hope that we can see the spirit—which is the actual mind—leaving the body. Let's go back and talk about the mind.*

The mind is the spirit; the spirit knows exactly what it's supposed to be doing. It's part of evolution to grow and become more efficient and to be able to use the deepest inner powers of our mind to create a better life. That's what we're supposed to be doing. However, we've taken a tangent on that because we keep swinging the pendulum from one extreme to another until we find balance. The pendulum always comes into balance eventually. Our evolution is about expanding, growing, contracting, and becoming more inward-looking.

Now contracting and becoming more insular doesn't necessarily mean that it has to be about war, pestilence, disease, epidemics, pandemics, or anything like that. It might be actually the opposite, if you think about it. We have this judgmental view, thinking we know it all, that when we're expanding and growing we're becoming people. How do we know that? We don't. It might be the complete opposite.

Looking at it that way, we can take expansion and growth as being war. It could be the innate knowledge that we're overpopulating, so therefore nature has to take its course in order to clear the world. We may decide that one will get AIDS, while another gets cancer. (We know that will sound weird, because we can create our own realities; let's say that's what we're doing—we're creating our reality.) Therefore, while that wipes 24 million people off the planet, we have the opposite end of the scale, with religion stating, "No, you can't do that. You have to keep procreating." Alternatively, we go into countries where they say, "You can only have one child." Talk about swinging the pendulum! It's multifaceted. There is no one way to evolve; there are many ways because we're not one-dimensional.

Evolution takes place in many dimensions. If we think of ourselves as multifaceted, multidimensional people, emotionally there's one set of developmental processes; mentally there's another series of growth processes; spiritually yet another set. However, spiritually doesn't mean "holier than thou"; nor does it imply going around with a begging bowl. It represents the integration of all aspects of a multidimensional human race, which we are.

Spirituality encompasses all of that. We're evolving through all of that, not just one aspect, because people, generally speaking, believe that spirituality means religiosity and praying to an entity that has control. The reality is we have control of our evolutionary state. We're driven by that and not always on a conscious level, sometimes on a very unconscious level. For instance, take a person who has abused their body (drug abuse and alcohol), and has harmed other people in ways that only hurts society, themselves, and the people whom they injured through contact. They may have stated that when they get to the age of thirty-three, they want to have a spiritual revelation if they have harmed anyone. For instance, they may have already asked for a revelation and stated this in spirit (before they came into the physicality of this world, because everything is manifested in spirit first before it comes into this world—as above, so below). Obviously, they have free will and choice to be able to choose whatever they want. They may have decided to take the experience so far. Let's say the person is going along in their life and states, "If I haven't made a difference in the world by the time I'm thirty-three, I want to have a spiritual revelation." They'll have their wake-up call at that time, whatever it may be. They turn themselves around and become an advocate for children with HIV, and they meet with people who can help their cause, and so on.

Who is to say that damage inflicted by people prior to their spiritual revelation didn't create spiritual revelations in those people whom they hurt? In actual fact, it's a very tightly woven universal energy that ebbs and flows on various energy levels—spiritually, mentally, sexually, physically, and emotionally, as well as on a quantum level. It is such a complex series of electrical impulses that affect all our lives, because we're all connected into that web, so to speak. We can exercise free will anytime, and when we do, we set off another set of electrical impulses that we've decided to be a part of in this complex web. Think of it as a spider's web, only it's spherical; within that sphere, you have all these webs as well. One person escapes, while another remains trapped. Who is to say how that's going to happen? We do. We create that to grow and become spirit in flesh, in order to be able to utilize all these wonderful powers of creation that we have. That's the bottom line of the expansion of the evolution of spirituality. We call it the evolution of spirituality, but in fact, it's evolution on a whole. Its sounds complex, but really it's all about free will and choice and whom we're going to connect with at any given time.

Think of us as a circle of people.

We're standing there with our hands behind our backs. One person decides he or she is going to touch another's shoulder and move into the center; the other person beside them says, "Okay, you have free will, but I'm going to follow you, because I want to see what that feels like. I want to experience that to see what 'that' is." Those two people go in. The person who is traveling might have family and may take their relatives with them. They go, and on that journey, they touch other people. Those families will touch other people. That person who's leading has decided at thirty-three years of age, "I'm going to have a spiritual revelation." That's just going to create a new set of electrical impulses that is going to draw in other people.

Therefore, you send that energy out, those other people are attracted to that energy, and in they come. Now these other people have fallen by the wayside, even though you may have done physical, mental, or emotional harm. Now they're going to attract another set of individuals, who might be just as physically abusive but have other attributes to offer them that might help break those chains within themselves.

What we're doing is we're breaking the chains of physicality, inasmuch as we're destroying those "harmful" effects that our ego has already set up, to become more spiritual in flesh, in order to integrate and become more powerfully creative in our world.

HELEN: Even though we have free will and choice, some people will say, "So if I don't want to grow spiritually, then I don't have to," when in fact we're all connected. If one person grows spiritually, we're all going to grow spiritually, even if it's in different ways.

JEN/UNIVERSAL SOURCE: Yes, of course you're going to grow because of the ripple effect. When you think about how energy works, for example, you throw a stone into a pond, and the water ripples. You throw another pebble into the pond, and you have those ripples interacting. Regardless if one person is in North America and someone else is in Australia, the ripple effect of those energies comes into play all the time. Think about 7 billion people on the planet. How could we not interact on an energy level? We do it all the time. That's how we think when we go somewhere and we see somebody we've never met before in our lives, and we ask, "Have I met you before?" Well, we were destined to meet at that particular time.

It's not really destiny; it's our power of creation. It isn't fatalist; it has nothing to do with fate, although there are people who are fatalists, and I don't mean to cross their boundaries. That's what they believe, and that's fine. However, if we take it a step further and say you've met someone, and you feel like you've known them all your life, it's because you've already interacted energy-wise. When you meet, it's lovely. You have this wonderful relationship, even if it only lasts for three seconds; it doesn't matter. Across the crowded room, you lock eyes with someone, and you feel as if you've known them all your life. Well, how do you know you're not passing information and energy right at that particular moment? We don't. We have no idea. We're surmising and theorizing but how do we know that's not what's actually happening? Just think when you pick up the phone without call display and know who it's going to be and say, "I knew you were going to call." You've already connected; you've already transferred telepathically, or whatever you want to call it. It doesn't matter because you're sharing energy and information in another way—other than speaking the human word and looking straight into the eyes of another human being—you're already connecting.

Therefore, if we take that to another level, we can say that it's energy reaching out, which has a ripple effect because it's stretching out. It reaches you, and you send the ripples back. We've taken that on a very simple level of the phone call; now Spirit wants to take it on a grander scale with an example.

How many people had dreams and knowledge of 9/11 before it happened? Hundreds said, "I had a dream about something really horrific." Two days later or a week later, 9/11 happened. You know you can call it mass hysteria, but many documented that they had dreams or thoughts of something horrific happening in their world that was going to affect them. It happened. You can disbelieve it all you like; those people have nothing to gain by being right. They know they had an experience of some sort that had a huge impact on their lives, because during that period before 9/11, there were many people who were anxious. You can call it a premonition or déjà vu or use other pigeonhole labels; the bottom line is, it's energy that's been sent out. We receive it as either negative or positive, and we try to make sense of that. It's very difficult, because our egos get in the way of that. If we just let go and allow that to filter, we would get the real answer. Again, that's the whole point of evolution. We're trying to tap into that energy on a constant basis, because we want to control and we want to know the outcome. Well, we can know the outcome and we can create the outcome, if we would just allow ourselves to expand.

HELEN: People will want to know how to expand.

JEN/UNIVERSAL SOURCE: *Learn how to be less rigid; allow each experience to show you something, no matter how small it might be. Awareness and being in the moment as best you can allow you to expand.*

Expansion comes from within. In order to expand, you have to be aware of who you are. It's back to that old adage "know thyself." If you know yourself, then you can expand your horizons, both internally and externally. Take, for example, a seasoned traveler who seems to have expanded her horizons because she's been exposed to many different cultures and walks of life. The same occurs within ourselves if we expand ourselves from within. Expanding ourselves from within involves looking at our belief systems and asking ourselves, "Is this as far as I want to go with this belief system? If so, then why? What is it serving if I only take my belief system this far?"

For instance, if we believe in Catholicism, it states that we are sinful, yet we can atone for our sins by asking a priest to be a mediator between God and ourselves, in order to have our sins forgiven. Then, the next day, we can sin again, only to atone for it yet again at a later date. We think we're securing a place in heaven for ourselves. We may only want to go that far with this belief system. However, in order to expand, we can ask the questions: Why do I only want to believe that? Why can't I believe that maybe I'm not in sin but I'm only experiencing life?

As soon as you start to open those horizons within yourself regarding your beliefs, then this completely new universe opens up within you. Your mind is starting to expand itself into different areas of knowledge; that's where the key is.

If you don't possess the knowledge and you can't find it within you, go seek it out. Go outside of yourself to find the knowledge, to see what others think. Ask yourself, "Do I believe that, or do I believe this instead? Can I function with this? What sits well within me?"

You then expand that belief and that horizon into the next step and so forth. That's what expansion is inside: expanding our minds, our beliefs, and our intellect as far as we can. Some of it may be hard, stressful work; we may be emotionally attached. Conversely, some of it may be easy. There are a million ways to look at it. There's not just a single, one-dimensional way; it's multifaceted and multidimensional. Compare it to centuries ago, when some people said the Earth was flat. They believed if you traveled too far across the ocean, you would fall off the edge of the planet. It took one brave soul to say, "I don't know if I believe that. I'm going to go out and see if I can find the edge of the world."

Of course, they never did. They just found more landmass, which led us to understand that our world is actually round. It's all about expansion. We wouldn't be where we are now without it. Hence, we could singularly, each one of us, expand our horizons by challenging the beliefs we have.

What are those beliefs serving? Do they serve? Can you find another way to live? Can you find another belief? Can you push the boundaries?

The more you expand your inner knowledge about who you are and what you're all about, the more you will know yourself. The more you know yourself, the more expansion happens. The more expansion happens, the more knowledge comes to you. It's an evolving circle.

We just have to look at science to see expansion in different areas—biology, geology, quantum physics, just to name a few. If we can expand our knowledge about the universe, then why wouldn't we be able to expand our knowledge about who we are?

HELEN: People are going to seek outside themselves and hear other people's thoughts and opinions (including ours). People may wonder what is true and what isn't, so let's define truth.

JEN/UNIVERSAL SOURCE: Truth is whatever it is you want to believe. It's up to you (the individual), to seek out your own truth. Truth will be what is for you at that moment in time but may not necessarily be what you might want to believe in ten years' time. On a deeper level, we all know what truth is for us. We know when we're deluding ourselves, because we keep convincing ourselves and justifying it to ourselves.

Your truth changes, depending on your belief systems and where you are (mentally, emotionally, or spiritually, for instance) in your life.

It's about questioning your truth and what you believe at that time. Do you think that there could be a greater truth? It's back to that truth within a truth within a truth.

HELEN: Let's reiterate. In the beginning of the book, Spirit talks about how truth resonates. However, what may be true for us today may not be true for us down the line. As we expand, our truth will change as well. Interestingly enough, you just mentioned something you've said to me for years—that there's a truth within a truth within a truth and so forth. In addition, years ago, you told me that Spirit stated that if we knew the truth, we wouldn't be able to handle it. I'm just wondering if we could expand on that.

JEN/UNIVERSAL SOURCE: Once you go on a spiritual path, you never turn back. It's impossible in a lot of ways, because the truth starts to settle within your being. We can feel it on the outside, and it's circulating really fast, and then it starts to slow down, and we can see it a bit; then it gets closer to our being and finally pops inside. We then have our "aha moment." It doesn't quite settle in the being yet; it has to find its place where it sits within us. It's like protons, electrons, and the nucleus in the atom—if you upset that balance, then that particular atom becomes something else. For example, if you take a proton away, you then change its molecular value. It either becomes something else or destabilizes. When we go through that, our molecules destabilize for a while, and we become destabilized as human beings, as our energy changes and manifests in a different way, as we learn another truth. That's the truth within a truth within a truth.

The interesting part about that is the core of that truth lies within us the whole time. We're just learning to manifest it from the inside out, even though we feel like it's coming from the outside in. It's actually within us all the time.

That whole aspect of us being a part of God or some omnipotent being is part of that truth within a truth within a truth—because we are creators in our own right.

If we truly knew how well we created, we wouldn't create what we're creating now. If we only knew the truth about the impact of every thought that we have, if we really knew the impact of every prayer we sent out or every healing hand we've placed upon a soul, a flower, or a tree. If we knew the true impact of how powerful we are as human beings, we would have a hard time handling that truth, because we have built into our egos that guilt and shame mechanism that would be overpowering. (In other words, realizing the negative we had created, which could have been prevented, and thus, as a result, creating overpowering guilt and shame within ourselves because of our actions.)

Hopefully, when we do recognize the truth regarding our powerfulness as a creator (and we do create on a daily basis), we will have removed that guilt and shame to such an extent that we can accept and move forward from where we've been to where we are going in a more enlightened and proactive way. If we're saying with our words, "I could just have killed them. They make me so angry …" that is an act of violence, a thought of violence. It's an energy of violence that has been put out into the universe. Imagine 7 billion people and only have half of them sending out messages of violence. What do you end up with? War, strife, greed, lack, guilt, shame, lust; we end up with all of those negative emotions. Spirit isn't saying we shouldn't experience them. We have experienced them for a long time, and maybe it's time to swing the pendulum the other way. It's not to swing the pendulum based upon righteousness that states "we're superior and you're inferior." But we are righteous in our own right, because we can create "right things"; "right doing"; and "right action," not based upon good or evil but based upon valuing our being, that of others, and our planet.

The bottom line is if you knew what you were creating—violent thoughts and actions that send out to our world the act of violence—would you be able to stop? Would you fight hard within your being to stop the acts of violence in your mind and how you perpetrate that crime within your being?

HELEN: Spirit has talked about the re-education of the planet spiritually. I was wondering if they could discuss that.

JEN/UNIVERSAL SOURCE: Spirit is talking about the re-education of value, integrity, and love—qualities that we can aspire to and attain by valuing ourselves primarily. When Spirit talks about the re-education of the planet spiritually, it doesn't mean religiously or even politically. It means the spiritual responsibility of each one of us—teaching ourselves, children, family, and those we encounter how to value ourselves and value others as well. It's about helping ourselves make the conscious decision to be a valued member of society. Valuing our being is making sure that everyone knows that you value your being; it's making sure they understand how to value your being. That means not allowing yourself to be abused. If we would stop enabling each other to create negative outcomes, would that not be considered valuing? We're encouraging each other to be successful in every shape of the word.

It means valuing who you are and having integrity and knowing within yourself that the spark is within you. Through that spark, you can do great things with your life, through the power of love (unconditional love with boundaries).

Valuing our being is understanding who we are. To educate ourselves is to know ourselves, so we know what we're capable of as spiritual human beings. We are quite capable of meeting those expectations and challenges for ourselves, spiritually speaking.

That's what re-education means.

Spiritually, it is about honoring the life—the life force that we have—and the ability to create in a positive way. If we understand that we can also create in a negative fashion and choose to surpass that (we choose to grow through that and maneuver our creation into a more positive way), then we're using our spirituality as a means to successfully create a positive outcome for all concerned, including oneself. Moreover, it can be done!

Once again, re-educating the planet, spiritually speaking, does not mean religiousness or faith. Although it can, if you are a deeply spiritual person and you're not going to use religion to be superior to another person, including what he or she believes. Then that's wonderful. As long as we're not using these as weapons to hurt other people. That's what re-education is about. It's about diplomacy; cooperation; helping each other, whether the person is good, bad, or indifferent; sharing; compromise; and all those wonderful aspects that lead up to the attribute of unconditional love.

HELEN: We've been talking a lot about valuing ourselves. However, for some, that may be a difficult concept. Let's start with the basics. What can we value about ourselves?

JEN/UNIVERSAL SOURCE: Start small, even if you cannot see anything beautiful about yourself. Start by valuing your amazing physique that through this toxic world we live in with all its pollution has the ability to try to adapt. That has been part of evolution since the time of hunters and gatherers, from all of those millions of years gone by, our bodies have adapted to our environment. That is what you do. That is a valuable asset to have as a human being.

If you think of some people who smoke all their lives and never get cancer, their bodies adapted. It is truly amazing. Think of the individual who lives in Africa and has to eke a meager existence out of the soil, which is literally just sand. Yet they do it. They've brought that amazing value to themselves. No matter what it is, if you can find value in everything that you do and everything you are, then that is amazing.

If you are vulnerable and you don't like it, accept the fact [that] you're vulnerable. That is a beautiful quality, and eventually you'll work away from the people who will take advantage of it and be with people who are like-minded, because like attracts like. You might also learn how to establish boundaries, thanks to those who have taken advantage of you and still keep your vulnerability, which is a truly great aspect of your being. Being vulnerable means you can feel and love, rather than shut out and ignore. Whatever we bring into our lives, we bring in order to help us learn and grow, to become fulfilled participants on this Earth plane. [All of this may sound hokey, but these are the words that I'm being given at this particular moment in time.] As we think about all of this, every human being has value. The value is—you are priceless.

Value your beautiful eyes, your characteristics, qualities of being able to be compassionate or to stand up for the underdog. You can value your physical being that is taking you through this journey that we call life. You can value the feeling of your own divine nature within your being (this too is valuable, since not everyone can feel this or believe in a human divine nature), so you may be able to go out in the world and touch one life. This one life brings in the six degrees of separation between everyone; the one life you may have touched experiences the ripple effect and goes on to touch someone in Australia, for example. There are so many unknown quantities about having a valuable part of our being, which we use to reach out and touch someone; we have no idea how valuable that can be. For example, you're just sitting there, and you feel someone is watching you. You turn and lock eyes, and you may never see that human being again in your life. For some reason, in that split instant, you were connected to that human being. How do we as a human race know you haven't made a huge difference in that human being's life? How do you know they didn't have value for you? Locking *eyes with someone and saying, "I see you," brings an immense amount of relief to a human being (Oh my God, I've actually been seen!). You may have felt love, that connection. Everyone has had moments—perhaps a split second—valuable moments, which have continued with us for the rest of our lives, and we don't know why. It connected with us and made us feel differently; it changed a course in our thinking and speaking in that particular moment in our lives. Therefore, whatever it is, hold on to it with both hands, and just know it really did mean something. At least say to yourself, "I valued that moment. It was valuable to me." Whether it was stopping to smell a flower, or valuing that you did something good and wonderful for another human being, or valuing something good someone else did for you.*

We can value our ability to love, create, and connect with intent to communicate; our ability to invent and realize our power of creation for the power of love; our divine nature; and our ability to love. Even when we have experienced dreadful pain, we still love.

HELEN: I think many may have difficulty in valuing their divine nature. For some, it's non-belief in that sort of thing; for others, it goes back to that feeling of disconnection. How can people feel less separate from God if they so choose?

JEN/UNIVERSAL SOURCE: It is all about the mind and where your mind is. Free will states you can choose to feel separate from God and continue on your way, or you can choose to feel connected. If your mind spends time running around scrambled, fearful, and anxious, how can it connect? Remember, your ego or frame of reference doesn't want you to connect, because if you do, then you won't need your ego or frame of reference in the same way. The ego was built into us to help us survive and progress. We needed to be able to find food, shelter, safety, warmth, and water.

We are always connected to our universe. We have all had moments and experienced split seconds where we feel absolutely connected, whether it's a beautiful flower, a puppy, a baby's smile, whatever it may be, even our amazing technology that saves people's lives!

We are all connected to a Higher Power; otherwise we wouldn't be able to create. We wouldn't have free will and choice, and we can create anything we want if we truly desire to. It's finding that awareness within. To state to ourselves in our mind, categorically, "We are connected on a daily basis, every second of the day."

The reason we feel separate from God is [because] we feel unlovable.

If you feel unlovable, it's your ego or frame of reference getting in the way, because we like to victimize ourselves or persecute others; we like to rescue others, since it allows us to feel worthy in some way.

Stop yourself and say, "I am breathing oxygen." If you live in the desert, state, "Look at this amazing sand and the life forms which can connect with the sand and live in adverse conditions." On the other hand, if you live in a temperate climate, [say,] "Look at the lovely green trees and fields."

Say to yourself mentally and emotionally and guide your ego or frame of reference out of the way by stating, "I am connected to a higher force. Each of us is special and perfect in our own right and has something to offer the world. We are trying to become spirit in flesh."

If you state this to yourself every day, you're going to end up believing it. A little piece of intelligence is going to spark in your brain and send all the synapses and neuropeptides throughout your body, which are going to create that loving experience within, which is called fulfillment.

HELEN: I think for some people that will be tough. They may not feel loved by God. I'm sure many people out there have been given mixed messages about God. I know for myself, having been raised Catholic, I was told that God loved us, but if you didn't live your life according to the Church, you could end up going to hell. I know I've questioned God's love. A person can say it and understand it intellectually, but knowing it on an emotional as well as a cellular level is another thing. How we can know and feel loved by God?

JEN/UNIVERSAL SOURCE: If you feel that you are unloved by God and considered unworthy by the universe (or however you see it in your mind), this is something only you can change, because it is a personal experience you have. If you want to keep victimizing yourself with it, then that is your free will and choice. However, you're never going to be happy or feel fulfilled (except on a negative basis).

Ask yourself on an emotional level, "If I have free will and choice, then why wouldn't I be loved by God?" In other words, God loves you enough to allow you to do whatever it is you want. Whether you're saint or sinner, you have free will and choice, which is evident through human action of abuse, intolerance, compassion, and love. We all have free will and choice, and that includes every person on the planet.

Free will isn't a setup for failure—it is a setup for success!

HELEN: I think we understand that, but to feel and know we're loved on a deep, cellular level is another thing. I think that's where I'm going with this question. You feel undeserving within yourself, just because of a dogma that has been taught. I understand it's a mind thing. However, if you were taught dogmas from an early age, then those beliefs will run very deeply. Spiritually, I was traumatized at the age of four, and

I truly believed there was something horribly wrong with me. If someone needs a savior to save your ass from hell, then it means you're not good enough; you're a sinner who needs redemption. I look back on my poor father, who passed away from cancer. He was terrified of dying, because he feared the other side and the possibility of hell. As adults, we can logically look at the mixed messages we've been taught regarding God's love; however, I feel many have been emotionally and spiritually stunted as a result. I guess it's about how one can shift the focus and release those beliefs within themselves.

JEN/UNIVERSAL SOURCE: Remember, we are all connected. You make the choice to feel separate from others and from God. If we are all creators and divine, connect with another who shares their divinity with others in a harmless way filled with love and honesty. It is love you feel separated from, the unconditional love of Spirit Divine.

Your knowing will grow, and you will have moments of feeling loved by God. Just by looking at the beauty of the world, you will remember how loved you are. By witnessing all the beauty around you with your own eyes, without judgment, you will see the divine within you. Cherish yourself and those you love with healthy boundaries, share the journey as best you can and know yourself.

If you are filled with hatred, there is a pinpoint of light of love within you, because it's the opposite end of the pole of love. It's just another form of love, really. Hatred comes from not understanding what you're looking at—which means you're fearful—and that is ego-based. If you didn't have your ego, you would love it (whatever it is). It's very simple, really, when you look at it; however, we like to make it very complex.

We love the thought that God doesn't love us, because it gives us something to strive for, but what you're really striving for is *yourself.*

You are looking for yourself.

You are looking for God, because God is in you all the time. Therefore, you are really looking for yourself and for the loving person you really are. The only way to find love of a divine nature is to *be loveable* and allow people to love you back! When you are ready to accept that "worthy love," it will come to you, and hopefully you won't reject or negate it, and just allow it in. If you think you're unworthy of love, you will end up creating unworthy love on a conscious or unconscious level.

Just think of all the different belief systems we generate within ourselves, due to societal thinking, which states that we aren't good enough. It's as if we're addicted to feeling unworthy. That's the true addiction—feeling unworthy; self-hatred. That's why we end up going into addicted phases, to release ourselves of that—whether it's dieting, overeating, drugs, alcohol, cigarettes, shopping, gambling, sex, or whatever the obsession may be. What we're really doing is swinging that pendulum so we know what we're not!

If you are kind and compassionate to others yet have balance and boundaries (loving yourself enough not to allow anyone to walk all over you), then you're not only helping yourself but also helping them to understand that they have this beautiful, universal soul within them that is equally lovable. It's when we get into competition with each other and with God that we become unwilling to see ourselves as lovable. Emotionally, as well as mentally, it's going to be a bit of a roller coaster ride. Mentally, that's where all your thought processes start regarding the concept of unlovingness and its unwillingness to see you are lovable. Emotionally, you're going to cry; you're going to weep for yourself. You'll say to yourself, "How could I have not seen how beautiful I was?" We don't say it enough to ourselves. We don't state, "How beautiful it is that I'm alive." Nor do we look at those wonderful feelings we have toward another human being, flower, animal, or tree. Who cares what it is that you love? It means you're alive and you're feeling. If this is the case, then you're a part of the universe, and if you're part of the universe, then you are a part of God.

Whether you believe it or not—you are a part of all that is.

Your happiness depends upon it.

However, there is no one specific mantra or affirmation one can use. What Spirit/higher self/soul is trying to say is there is no real answer, because each individual is unique in his or her own right. Each person will find his or her own way—whether through a mantra, closing their eyes and meditating, going for a walk, watching an inspirational movie, reading inspirational books, or volunteering. There are so many ways to express yourself in a loving manner, so you can understand that you have to be lovable because you're a part of the whole universe. What Spirit is trying to say is that you have to find what fits for you. It could be just about anything, as long as it doesn't harm you or another human being (or anything else in the universe).

HELEN: During a private conversation (via Spirit), I asked how we know if God loves us or not. Please restate the answer.

JEN/UNIVERSAL SOURCE: Think about the intelligence of our cells; each cell knows what's expected. Through unconditional love, it keeps creating itself repeatedly, in order for us to manifest our beings. Then there are cells, which create dis-ease and difficulties with illnesses; they mutate and speed up, or they mutate and slow down because of the way we think, breathe, eat, drink, feel, and move around in our world. Either we can make ourselves feel well or feel unwell, based upon how we think and how we process our emotions. For instance, if we're angry in our mind, our whole body is angry. If we're upset in our mind, our whole body is upset. When people find out about cancer when it's too late, it might be because they haven't listened to their bodies until it's too late, or maybe they did listen, but they ignored it due to fear.

How do we know God loves us? Because our body keeps trying to do the right thing by us, it keeps trying to create a beautiful being for us to live through. In order for it to do all of this, it surely has to love. If it loves and it is born out of love and it's there for us to manifest and create, then does this not say something? Does this not say how much love there actually is in the universe? How do we know God loves us? Because we are still here and still creating.

Think about the different ways we believe in God, such as those who believe God is a vengeful God. If that's the case, does it not stand to reason that we would all be obliterated by now? There are those who believe they're the chosen ones (and rightly so, according to their religion), while thinking the rest of us are schmucks. If that's the case, and God hates the rest of us that much, then why has It not gotten rid of us by now? There will be some who will say, "Well, isn't that what war and pestilence are doing?"

Yet, we're the ones who created war and other horrors by interfering with the way we perceive each other negatively and by destroying our Earth the way we do, for instance, with nuclear waste. We have the ability to create, and yes, we've created in a negative way, but if God were angry with us, we would all be gone by now.

We can also look at God as being benevolent. This also could be true, because benevolence means God is a loving God that loves always.

Every religion and holy book talks about free will and choice. When we are loved unconditionally, we are allowed to do whatever we want to do, without judgment or criticism. The non-judgment and non-criticism give us the right to live and to experience. Hence, we've been given this planet as a gift, and we've been given each other as a gift. We have a beautiful world we live in, that we only catch glimpses of, because more often than not, we're not in the present. Yet, we are still here. This says volumes. It says that God doesn't judge and loves us for what and who we are and allows us to experience.

HELEN: We're not trying to convert anyone, but those who don't believe in God yet lack love within themselves are going to wonder how this applies to them. What does God have to say to someone who is an atheist and thinks this is all just a bunch of crap?

JEN/UNIVERSAL SOURCE: Wonderful! *They are exercising their free will and choice to believe what they will. Their experience will be the testament of love or hate, and whether they choose to experience love or hate is entirely their choice. Of course, we would love for them to experience love, and possibly their own blueprint of their lives here will incorporate that at some point. However, it is their choice.*

CHAPTER SEVENTEEN

A WORD FROM OUR SPONSOR

HELEN: IT WOULDN'T BE ME if I didn't ask God if It had anything else to say. I'm just wondering if there's a message that God wants to give the world in general terms or just impress upon us.

Drum roll, please ... and now a word from our sponsor!

JEN/UNIVERSAL SOURCE: In the name of everything holy, quit fucking fighting! Have you no idea how totally useless violence is? Energy is exerted beyond the means, where speaking in gentle tones and accepting the opposites of you as part of the process of being human will allow a society to flourish as it shares its knowledge and skills.

Well, that would be one of them. I can only give you a personal perspective, as I ask the universe, God, or however you understand it in your own heart what would be the best thing that could ever happen.

It would be to love each other enough to allow balance and joy into everybody's lives.

This unique thinking that we have in this day and age that we have to suffer in order to survive or to appreciate—I'm not judging anyone else's thinking, but I'm just saying that if we continue on that kind of thinking, then we're saying that God doesn't deserve to have happiness through us. If we say that, then what are we doing? Why do we need to suffer in order to evaluate in order to know? We don't if we were all raised in a spiritual environment. It wouldn't have to include God's name by any stretch of the imagination because you can still be spiritual and still be atheist, agnostic, or any of those things, yet still be a spiritual human being. If we choose to think more on a spiritual level, and that means emotionally and mentally being informed and allowing our neural networks to rebuild in a positive and loving manner, if we were raised in that environment, then we wouldn't think we needed to suffer.

It's to allow ourselves to understand the true meaning of the laws of cause and effect, action and reaction, proactive and reactive, or however you want to call it. (It's all saying the same thing.) It's the basic laws of consequence as to what we want to choose for ourselves and others.

When I'm talking to the universe or God, it has never changed; it's always about loving yourself enough to love another person—loving yourself enough to be proactive and joyful, and loving the other, whoever is beside you, enough to allow them to be proactive and joyful.

We are truly connected to one another. I think that's the big thing—we are all fragments of the same mirror, but we're not fragmented; we're all part of it. If we can truly bring that into our hearts and understand (but not from an egotistical point of view) that we're all connected. We're even connected to the Saddam Husseins, the Osama Bin Ladens of this world; the reason we don't like that is because we're placing judgment on it instead of stating: that person has become that way because of their neural network and what choices they have made throughout their lives.

We can judge it all we like, but the fact remains the same. We were all children at one time. If we go back and say that we had a good childhood and all the rest of it, while some things weren't too happy, we can change that now. We have children today in this day and age that have no control over anything, and we don't give them that control, because we never give them the spiritual tools—the mental and emotional tools to be able to make choices by giving them many solutions for them to choose from. (By helping them reinstate that neural network that was so naturally present for them at a young age.) So why do we allow that to continue?

I guess really that's what the universe or I'm saying personally is: why are we allowing that to continue if we are all one as the universe/God, the Creator, or however you know it in your heart has always stated (even before Jesus)? We are all connected; we are all one. If we can understand that we are connected to what we perceive as the lowest of lows; the worst of the worst; the cruelest of the cruel; the pedophiles; murderers; dictators; the abusers of men, women, children, and animals—if we can understand that it's because they have not been given the tools to flip the switch to allow their beauty to come out, then we might get a better grasp on why we're all connected. We're all connected to help one another in one way or another. We can't insulate ourselves and be in a little pigeonhole, never knowing and constantly running on fear, because the fear will eventually destroy some of us. It will definitely kill some of us, and [that DNA], if there's children involved, will keep itself until such time as somebody says, "Wait a minute; it doesn't have to be this way."

HELEN: If we don't feel good enough, and as a result we don't believe we deserve, then we're going to create the same pain repeatedly, and that is to hurt each other to get what we think we deserve because we think we're entitled.

JEN/UNIVERSAL SOURCE: If we are willing to destroy our world, then we are willing to destroy ourselves, our children, our children's children, and so forth.

Therefore, we have the sins of the forefathers.

In summary to it all, in order to break bad habits, one has to relearn and rethink.

If you become consciously aware of your actions and thoughts, you are going to get tired, feel exhausted, and it's going to take a lot of effort. You're going to want to fall back, but don't.

Don't fall back into the ego-based habits.

Keep thinking about how joyful you're going to be when you don't have to carry that burden around in order to stay and maintain who you are. You think that changing habits is going to be difficult; the reward is spiritual enlightenment.

The reward is an inner joy, an inner love.

The reward is a better place to live in—a more peaceful world.

The rewards that we're seeing right now are all ego-based: we see fighting, war, a need for organizations to keep a watch out for human deprivation. This is all ego-based, reactive thinking.

If you think that working on spiritual enlightenment is difficult, wait till you see yourselves twenty years from now, when you have coronary artery disease, liver disease, emphysema, and the like, because you've overindulged, egotistically speaking, in your ego-based needs. Watch how one side of the world is in deprivation, while the other side is in affluence.

This is all the imbalance.

In summary, don't be afraid of working toward spiritual enlightenment—it's an amazing place, because insights come, and they stay with you.

Ego-based insights come, and they destroy you.

HELEN: I think, with these concepts, people will be able to step out of the illusion that they cannot be at the God level. We can. We are. It's about equality in every sense—with ourselves, with each other, with our environment, and with God. I know I've bought into the illusion.

However, for all the naysayers, I would like to take it to the extreme. Let's say for argument's sake that God may not even exist, and life is an illusion. Just as a dream seems real, it's only a thought. Quantum physics states we are 99.99 percent empty space. Let's hypothesize that this is all a figment of our imagination, and it's only a thought. Where does the thought come from? If there is no God, and this is all an illusion, and it's only a thought, then that thought has to come from somewhere.

JEN/UNIVERSAL SOURCE: A thought is intelligence in its own right, because it has the ability to create. Just as much as stars are born, thoughts are born in the same way—it is electrical impulses. Electrical impulses run through our universe, beyond, and into other solar systems and so on. It's this spark of life that has no option but to manifest itself in some way. Why does it manifest itself? It wants to be known. Thought is exactly the same thing; thought wants to be known, and that's why it surfaces in your mind and surfaces as this, what we call an illusion. As scientists say, we're 99.99 percent empty space. Well, that space isn't empty, because it's like a cosmic soup. If you think about it, there are all different kinds of carbons floating around in that soup.

If you use the example of chicken broth, you might say it's soup, while someone else may say that it's just a base. It's not just a base; there are all sorts of things going on in a microscopic level inside of that soup. The cosmos and the universe is exactly the same; there's all sorts of things going on in that soup. Yes, there is 99.9 percent empty space, but there is .01 percent of matter. That matter is born out of that space. In that space, you have electrical impulses that charge and bounce off each other that become matter. I don't know how else to explain that, because that's what I'm seeing in my head. If we take it on a grander scale, intelligence is thought, and thought is intelligence in some form or another. We have the idea that intelligence means something as a high IQ of 160; that's not necessarily so. Anything that is thought becomes matter; it's created into matter.

For example, an apple blossom starts as a flower. It creates itself into an apple, a piece of fruit. Now, when it's a flower, it's only thinking about that. It's thinking, I'm going to manifest myself into an apple. *It then goes ahead and does it. A pear doesn't grow out of it. It thinks about being an apple, and it becomes an apple. It first thinks about it. It's like the tree. When the tree is planted in the ground as a seed, it's a seed. The thought is already within the seed that it is going to become a tree. Depending on weather conditions and the like, it will determine how big and bushy the tree will grow and how well it will be, because of its surroundings.*

Thought and intelligence are the same thing—it's affected by its surroundings. So how it's going to create will be dependent upon the soup that it is in and how mixed up it gets in that soup. So that's how you know—whether you believe in God or not, or if you just believe in the Big Bang Theory. I think it's because we have this need to believe in something greater and bigger than us. That is us—we are the creators. We've created all of this!

If you look at each country in every continent, there is animal, aquatic, and plant life that is not indigenous to the area, because we have brought it from other areas, thinking it would also be able to survive there. We bring it (it's a thought), we plant it, and it grows—it becomes an intelligent life force in itself.

We are God; we are the ones that create, and we are part of that whole system—it's that six degrees of separation. We're all connected. We're all just one big fabric of God, the universe, or however you understand it in your own heart.

You don't necessarily have to believe in a Divine Being. To me, it is divine enough to be able to create. We talk about gods and how they create—that's what we do!

We do it every day. We cannot see that we are creating and that we are God in our own right.

That's the real illusion—we do not believe that we are God in our own right, with our own thinking, and that our thoughts turn into creations.

Lightning Source UK Ltd.
Milton Keynes UK
UKOW01f0722291216

290947UK00001BA/299/P

9 781491 845585